Small Business
FORESIGHT
The Future of Your Business

Verne Wheelwright, Ph.D.

ALSO BY VERNE WHEELWRIGHT

It's Your Future… Make it a Good One!

The Personal Futures Workbook

Small Business Foresight Workbook

YOUR Workbook

Oreo and Erin (with Erin King)

Copyright ©2019 by Verne Wheelwright

Published by Personal Futures Network

1917 Guava Circle, Harlingen, TX 78552

verne@personalfutures.net

smallbusinessforesight.com

ISBN: 978-0-9892635-7.3

Library of Congress Control Number: 2019944776

Printed in the United States of America

Contents

Figures

Figure 9.3- Threats at three levels— Local, National and International.

Figure 9.4- The Futures Wheel.

Figure 9.5- A basic business Futures Wheel showing spaces for the first level of forces.

Figure 9.6- From the basic Futures Wheel, extend outward to create another ring, or second level of impacts.

Figure 9.7- The Futures Wheel expanded to another level of impacts.

Figure 9.8- You can build a Futures Wheel from any of the domains of your business.

Figure 9.9- In this example, the Futures Wheel is expanded from one node of the Operations domain to explore some of the options available to the Shipping and Receiving department.

Figure 9.10 - This Futures Wheel adds technology that is still in the future, but could change the way you or your competitors do business.

Figure 10.1- The cone of uncertainty is the space between the best and worst plausible projections.

Figure 11.1- Scenarios focus primarily on high-impact, high-probability events, while wild card scenarios are based on low-probability, high-impact events.

Figure 11.2- An example of a scenario worksheet showing high impact, high probability events for a small business.

Figure 15.1- A worksheet for developing a vision for a small business.

Figure 16.1- Some strategies for a one-person business.

Figure 16.2- Strategies for a small business of any size.

Figure 16.3- Long term strategies that will apply through all stages of the business including the exit stage.

Figure 17.1- A few strategies for a one-person business. Very brief, but provides a list to guide the business into the future.

.Figure 17.2- A blank Action Plan worksheet, from the Small Business Foresight Workbook.

Figure 17.3- An example of how a small business might document a ten year Action Plan.

Figure 17.4- Backcasting can help build the sequence of actions necessary for your Action Plan.

Figure 18.1- The six forces of change within your business can each be an area of vulnerability.

Figure 18.2- A worksheet to help identify and deal with gaps in your business.

18.3- A few examples of unintended consequences.

Figure 19.1- Positive and negative wild cards to help you consider possible future events.

Figure 19.2- Examples of potential high impact events and a few possible solutions.

Figure 19.3- An example of a simple plan for dealing with high impact events that you don't want to occur in your business.

Acknowledgements

More than fifty people from the worldwide community of professional futurists have contributed to the development of this book. Many others, from the authoring community, also offered suggestions and encouragement. There is not enough room here to acknowledge all of them, but some people spent considerable time and effort. Dr. Fern Evitt reviewed and edited the manuscript, a huge contribution. Gary Hamel and Kurt Callaway proofread and offered corrections across the entire manuscript. Jim Burke offered valuable suggestions and comments throughout, as did Thomas Mengel. Many others offered considerable encouragement, which was greatly appreciated.

My wife and best friend, Betty, endured my distraction and hours at the computer while creating this book. She kept our lives running smoothly throughout, helped me with decisions, and kept me healthy.

This book is dedicated to Betty.

Introduction

mall business is different.

Because small business is different from big business, some methods and tools used by large organizations work well for small business. Some don't.

The methods that professional futurists use to anticipate and plan for the future have been used very effectively by big business for decades, but it is necessary to *apply* those methods differently in small business, and that's what this book is about. This book will show you how to recognize the forces of change in your business— even if your business is just you (as my small business is, and has been for years, — just me!)

What qualifies me to tell you how to develop and apply foresight in your business? I have worked in and owned small businesses for over 50 years. My export business grew to exceed $5 million in annual sales before I started reducing the business in order to go back to school to study Foresight and Futures Studies. I received a Master's degree from the University of Houston in Studies of the Future, and a Ph.D. from Leeds Metropolitan University for my research and thesis, *Personal Futures: Foresight and Futures Studies for Individuals*.

I am a professional futurist. I have spoken to large and small groups, led workshops, and taught university classes in many different parts of the world. My books and workbooks have been published, translated, sold, and downloaded around the world. My book, *It's YOUR Future... Make it a Good One!* was awarded the "Most Important Futures Work" first place award by the Association of Professional Futurists.

I wish this book, *Small Business Foresight,* had been available fifty years ago! The tools and methods of foresight—scenarios, visioning and strategic planning would have been very useful, but were simply not available. Today, although these methods are successfully used by large organizations and governments around the world, they have not previously been made adaptable to small business. The intent of this book is to correct that by introducing a system of methods specifically intended for use by small businesses to anticipate the future, choose a preferred path to the future and achieve that chosen future.

Small business is personal. The United States Census Bureau and the Small Business Administration now have a category, "Nonemployer Businesses". This category has risen from 15.4 million non-employer firms in 1997 to 24.3 million non-employer firms in in 2015. Non-employer firms can be reasonably defined as single person businesses. The owner does everything! Technology and the Internet have allowed small businesses to conduct business around the world, at low cost. In the 1970s a telephone call from the U.S. to Seoul, South Korea cost over $12.00 per minute! Today, email, voice and video are free nearly everywhere.

If you have read *It's YOUR Future... Make it a Good One!* you will find many parallels, because in both books, the methods are the same. *It's YOUR Future...Make it a Good One!* is written for individuals and families, while *Small Business Foresight* is written for owners and managers of small businesses. Yes, the two books are similar (and some paragraphs identical) — in part because small business is personal.

The system of methods and tools you will learn about in this book is not complex. You will use a simple, step-by-step approach to understanding and preparing for the future, and it works! Here's a little history of futures methods, lifted from the first chapter of *It's YOUR Future...Make it a Good One!*

For thousands of years of written history, people have wanted to know about the future. They consulted witches, fortune tellers, palm readers and astrologists, but to no avail. Finally, in the twenty-first century, most of them gave up. In this electronic age, people finally realized that no one can really tell them the future. But ...

Now it is possible. It is possible to understand and anticipate some the future! It is even possible to influence or change the future. Not all of the future, but enough to be valuable.

In the 1950s and 1960s, think tanks and academics developed theories about anticipating the future. What was it that the think tanks found that the wizards and fortune tellers of earlier centuries had not? The answer seems so simple. The fortune tellers had focused on THE future, assuming there was only one fixed, or preordained future.

The twentieth-century thinkers changed that main assumption. They were convinced that the future is not predetermined. That realization altered everything about the way we see the future. Now, it became obvious that if the future is not fixed or predetermined, then more than one future must be available.

Finally, they realized that it is possible to change the future through the actions we take in the present. This was a whole new way to look at the future!

Military and business organizations took those theories seriously and developed practical methods to explore and prepare for the future. The methods proved successful and spread into businesses and governments around the world. Royal Dutch Shell developed scenarios that anticipated the OPEC crisis of the 1970s, to their great benefit. Futurists wrote scenarios for South Africa that changed the expected future of that nation and led to a peaceful exchange of power. Futurists raised the alarm of the millennium bug in computer systems. Business and government responded in time to avoid a disruption.

To business, the military, and governments worldwide, the concept was clear. Methods for anticipating the future work.

Today, futures or foresight methods are now practiced around the world. As the result of recent research, these same methods have now been successfully scaled down to fit the life of one-person, one family, or one small business. Anyone. This book will introduce you to futures methods and how they work; then it will lead you, step-by-step, through the futuring process in just three parts.

1. Look at your business and where it is now

2. Explore potential futures with scenarios

3. Create a strategic plan for the future—the future you want for your business.

As you follow this futuring process, you will be practicing the same methods and techniques that futurists have applied successfully for large organizations over the past several decades.

It really is that simple.

Verne Wheelwright

verne@personalfutures.net

CHAPTER 1

Small Business and the Future

Concept

Small business is different! It is *not* the same as big business.

First, there is a matter of scale. Tools, techniques, and methods that work for large business may not work as well for small business simply because of the differences in size. In my opinion, that is the case with thinking about, anticipating, and planning for the future.

The methods and techniques involved in understanding or anticipating the future have been employed very successfully in large businesses around the world. Those methods and techniques scale down very effectively for small business, but because of the differences between large and small, the methods work best when *applied differently* to small businesses.

Second, big business (in the U.S. a business with more than 500 employees, according to the U.S. Small Business Administration) hires professionally trained and educated people for nearly all non-labor positions, and certainly in those positions relating to management. Small businesses are frequently owner-managed, and the owners may or may not be proficient in all the skills that are needed to manage a business. In some areas of the enterprise, small business owners are learning on the job.

If you are in a small business, you are not alone. There are more than 29 million small businesses in the United States (2017), and nearly 24 million small businesses *with no employees*. At the other end of the scale, just over 18 thousand firms in the U.S. employ more than 500 people.

Everyone wants to know the future!

Why do we study the future? For thousands of years, people have wanted to know about the future. They wanted to know their "fortune". They went to soothsayers, witches, fortune tellers of all types--anybody who could tell them or *might* be able to tell them about their future.

Thinking about the future began to change in the middle of the 20th century. In the 1950s, and early 1960s, several think tanks started focusing on what could be known about the future. Their clients, large businesses, the military, governments, all wanted to have a better view of what the future could be.

These think tanks arrived at several conclusions and three of the most important of those conclusions are the foundation of what futurists believe and practice today.

First: The Future Cannot Be Known

The future cannot be known, but we can make some very good educated guesses about the future and that's what futurists do, make educated guesses about the future.

Second: The Future Is Not Predetermined

That's the big one—for thousands of years, people have felt that the future was preordained or predetermined, that there was only one future. They felt they just had to find the right fortuneteller to tell them what that future might be.

If it is true that the future is not predetermined that means many things—most important, it means that more than one future is available. If more than one future is available, then it follows that some futures are going to be better than others.

This concept, that the future is not predetermined, led to the development of the Scenario Method. Royal Dutch Shell was an early proponent of developing "scenarios"[3]— stories about plausible or possible futures. Scenarios that the Shell team developed anticipated the formation of OPEC (Organization of Petroleum Exporting Companies, a cartel organized in 1960), and the successes of Shell's strategies for dealing with that event brought scenario development to the attention of organizations around the world. Individuals from the Shell team were later involved in the development of the "Mont Fleur" scenarios[4] which are credited with influencing the peaceful transition of South Africa to representative government and away from apartheid. The Mont Fleur scenarios were conducted and presented in full view of the public and the world, demonstrating the value of the scenario method.

And that brings us to the third conclusion.

Third: The Future can be Influenced by the Actions of Individuals or Organizations in the Present.

We can influence the future!

You may find that hard to believe.

In my workshops, very often people ask me, "Can we really influence the future?" My answer is YES!

You do it every day.

Think about that.

If in the next hour, you make plans with friends and meet for coffee or drinks or dinner, this evening…you have changed your future. Otherwise you would be doing something that you normally do every evening.

If you make an appointment with the dentist or a doctor, for 2 weeks, a month, two months away from now…. you've changed your future. If you make plans or reservations for a vacation for yourself and your family for next summer, you have changed your future.

If we can change the future in the short term, then *why not change the future in the long term*? And that's exactly what futurists believe. We believe that you can influence your future by the decisions that you make today. If you decide to start or acquire a business, you will certainly change your future!

What does all this have to do with small business? Most people are aware that large businesses use the tools and methods of foresight, including scanning, trend analysis, scenario development, vision development, and strategic planning, but there are substantial differences between large organizations and small businesses.

I want to emphasize that exactly the same tools and methods of foresight used by large businesses are employed by small businesses. These methods are scalable, so the methods are just as effective for small businesses as they are for large businesses. The difference is that these methods are most effective when they are *applied* differently to small business. This is true in part because small business is more *personal* than most large businesses.

More personal? What does that have to do with anything?

The answer to that question varies around the world, so let's start with some simple definitions. In Australia, a small business is under 15 employees, in the European Union less than 50 employees, and in the United States less than 500 employees. Medium-size businesses in those three geographic areas range from 200 to 500 employees. Very small businesses sometimes classified as micro-businesses would include from 1 to 10 employees, again varying in different countries and regions.

The difference is more than scalability. The methods we will explore throughout this book are very scalable, but there are other, important differences between large businesses and small businesses. For example, managers in large organizations are usually experienced professionals, working in their areas of expertise. In small businesses, owners are frequently managing ALL areas of the business, including areas where they have limited experience. Many owners are learning new skills on the job.

At the same time, small business owners may be personally at risk for financial losses in a business that is not only their primary source of income, but also represents the family's wealth.

In short, small business owners have personal responsibility and risk where corporate managers have positions, or jobs. A small business owner who fails, not only loses his or her source of income, but may also lose a lot more.

What Is Small Business Foresight?

Small business foresight is a system for understanding, anticipating, and dealing with the future. This system is composed of several methods, techniques and tools. These are the same methods used successfully by professional futurists worldwide in large organizations, including businesses, governments, military and nongovernment organizations. In this book, we will explore how these methods can be successfully scaled down and applied to small business. For clarity and simplicity, the book is divided into three sections.

I-   Look at Your Business and Where You Are Now

This section focuses on the past and present of your business and understanding the forces of change that will (or may) impact your business.

II-   Explore Potential Futures with Scenarios

This is the core—the future. Here you will use whatever you learned about your business and the forces of change to explore plausible and possible futures—the good, the bad, the unexpected, and the future to which you aspire.

III-   Create the Future—the Future You *Want* for Your Business

In this section you will learn how to visualize the future you want for your business, develop strategies to achieve that vision, then lay out a plan to execute those strategies. Effective strategic planning built on a foundation of understanding the future and anticipating change.

SMALL BUSINESS FORESIGHT

This book really is about the future of your business. That may sound a little like a fantasy, but it is about the methods you can use to anticipate and prepare for the future of your business. This book will help you understand your small business in terms of where it is now and what the future of that business can be, and how to develop your business into what you want it to be.

All of this is based on proven methods of foresight that have been used by businesses around the world for decades.

To help you with the methods and tools described in these pages, there is a workbook, (Small Business Foresight Workbook) available at *www.smallbusinessforesight.com* and at *www.Amazon.com*.

Look at your business-
Where are you now?

Whether your business has been in existence for years, or is alive only in your imagination, this section will first focus on the present— where your business is *now*.

You will identify and explore the forces of change that are likely to impact or affect your business in the present and in the future. You will begin identifying future events that have a both a probability of occurring and a strong impact on your business, either positive or negative.

At the end of this section, you will learn to use a tool employed by futurists around the world, the Futures Wheel.

We start by examining the development of a business.

CHAPTER 2

Stages of Business Development —

A Guide to the Future

Concept

As we age, humans go through a number of different stages in their lives (Infant, Child, Adolescent, Young adult, Adult, Middle age, and Independent). These stages are in our genes and have been observed for thousands of years. So, we humans age linearly. Every minute, we grow older, and move toward another biological stage.

Businesses also progress through stages, but the stages are *not* related to the passage of time. The movement from one stage to another represents accomplishment or change in the business, often related to growth.

Stages of Business Development

If you search Google for business stages, there are a lot of lists. The following list of stages is in general agreement with most of them, and fits well with my own experiences.

1- Concept Stage

The first stage of a business is the "concept" stage. This is when the *idea* for a new business occurs. This idea or concept may be a new invention, a different way to do business (clicks versus bricks), a new design, something simple and unique (like email), or something that could change the world and the way we live (solar power), or simply converting a hobby into a business.

In this stage, you will be asking yourself if this could really be a business, and what would you have to do to make your idea viable and profitable.

2- Planning Stage

In this stage, you will seriously test your concept and model on paper (or in a computer) and plan how to make it work. You will decide what you really need in terms of capital, location, equipment, people, and legal structure. You will develop an understanding of the industry, the market, and the competition. At the same time, you will identify potential customers, consider market research, develop a marketing plan and a business plan, and begin the search for adequate capital.

What do you *want* your business to be in the future, say 10 years from now? Will it be a unicorn (a business that experiences exponential growth), worth a billion dollars or more? Will it be nearly the same in ten years as when you started the business (a shop, service, franchise or other business that is not expected to grow substantially) an enterprise that you can manage on your own? Something in between?

The real question here is, "What do you *want* your business to be or to achieve?" To answer that question, you will need to define your long term interests in this business and consider your exit strategy. What kind of an organization do you want, now and in 10, 20, 30 years from now?

3-Startup Stage

Your business now exists. You are testing your concepts in the real world with a location, staff, product or service, and customers. This may include outfitting a facility, for 1 or for 100, buying or building inventories, making sales, and receiving orders and payments.

4-Struggling/Surviving Stage

You are adapting your business to the real world, where your business is accepted as a viable business, but struggling to grow and become profitable, to do more with less, to find more hours in each day, to reach the breakthrough that brings a sense of security and longevity.

Many businesses never grow beyond this stage.

5-Growth Stage

Sales and revenues are increasing. Additional employees or contractors may be added to carry the additional work loads. Adding new customers. This growth can be gentle or exponential, but if you want exponential growth, it is critical that you prepare for it.

6- Maturity Stage

The business is established and maintaining its balance, protecting the organization and product lines that brought the business to this level. Growth has slowed, in some cases because the organization has grown so large that exponential growth in no longer feasible.

7-Decline Stage

Shrinking profits, shrinking sales, aging systems or equipment. The firm may lose its competitive edge or the entire industry may decline. Often this stage is the result of external change, including product obsolescence. Horse-drawn carriages, kerosene lanterns, fax machines and typewriters are examples of products that were still good products when they were made obsolete by new technology.

8-Exit Stage

The point at which owners sell or give away majority control of the business. The time to think about the exit stage is during the planning stage. How long do you want to run or be involved with this business? The rest of your life? Do you want to take the business public? Do you want to build the business for sale to a bigger company? Turn it over to your children? Or simply close the doors some day? What is your exit strategy?

Sell, transfer or close. An exit can be taken at any stage.

Below is a table that briefly summarizes the stages of growth.

Stages of Business Development

Stages	Descriptions of each stage
Concept	The idea for a business.
Planning	Seriously testing your concept on paper (or the computer) and planning how to make it work. Deciding what you really need in terms of capital, location, equipment, people, and legal structure. Understanding the industry and the competition. Developing a business plan.
Startup	The business now exists. Testing your concepts in the real world with a location, product or service, and customers.
Struggling-Surviving	Adapting, accepted as a viable business, struggling to grow and become profitable. Some businesses do not survive this stage.
Growth	Sales and revenues are increasing. Additional employees or contractors may be added to carry the additional work loads. Adding new customers.
Maturity	Established. Maintaining balance.
Decline	Shrinking profits, shrinking sales, aging systems or equipment. Firm may lose competitive edge or industry may decline.
Exit	Sell, transfer or close. An exit can be taken at any stage.

Figure 2.1- Stages of Business Development.

Dealing with the Business Stages

We started this chapter with a description of the various business stages, but what do you *do* with a stage? You deal with it, and here are some thoughts about dealing with each of these stages.

First, let's explore those nine stages in a little more detail

Concept Stage

What is your idea for your business? A product? A service? An entirely new concept? An existing business or franchise? Can this idea be built into a profitable business?

Your idea for a business doesn't have to be revolutionary, but it should be clearly defined and thought through. This should be an idea you love and can explain easily to others—and they should just as easily understand it.

Planning Stage

Who will do this?

Who will found this business? One individual or two or more partners? Who will provide legal and accounting advice or services?

There are advantages and disadvantages in any choice. Partnerships can be very effective, but it is important that partners be chosen *very* carefully and expect to work together for ten or more years, possibly until the sale or retirement of the business.

- How well do you know your potential partner(s)? Their spouse(s)?
- Do you trust your partner(s) with everything you own?
- Does your partner have skills or knowledge that complement your own?
- Do you have a written and signed partnership agreement?

At the very least, you should decide upon or create the following during the planning stage. You may want to talk to a lawyer or CPA about legal, tax and accounting areas.

- Organizational structure
    - Sole proprietor
    - Partnership
    - Limited liability company
    - Corporation— S Corporation? C Corporation?
    - Who will manage the business? If more than one partner, what is the division of responsibilities?
- Legal considerations

Patents, trademarks, trade secrets, and copyrights should be documented and filed.

Contracts between partners, business associates and key employees should be completed and signed.

- Financial accounting system
    - A bookkeeper to record all financial transaction, issue invoices, bills and checks.
    - An accountant to review all transactions and monitor bank accounts.

Planning for the future

- Financial plan (business plan). Can this business pay the bills and make a profit? When?
- Strategic plan. What strategies will you implement?
- Marketing plan. What is your plan to sell your products or services? Who should be your customers/clients? Who is your competition? What is your marketing area? (Local, regional, national, international)?

If you don't have the patience or time to create these three plans (marketing, financial, strategic) at this point, you should ask yourself if you really want to start this business at this time. These plans are important and will determine the success (or not) of your business and how quickly you achieve it.

This is also a good place to ask yourself about your expectations for your business. A great deal of emphasis has been placed on growth. Growth in a business creates excitement, but fast growth can be very demanding of owners, personnel and cash flow, whether your business is a retail or wholesale store, a professional business, a local service business, a brokerage, or a technology business. The fact is that growth in any type of business may be exhilarating, but it will also be demanding.

How big do you want your business to grow? How big could or should the business grow? How much time do you want to spend in the business once it is up and running? How much risk do you want to take? How many employees do you want to manage? How much time do you want for your personal and family life? These are questions you should answer before you start making commitments.

Startup Stage

You are open for business!

Each type of business has different requirements. They may all be small businesses, but a retail store of any kind (clothing, restaurant, hardware) will have different requirements from a business offering services in homes or business offices or a business that requires little more than a computer and an Internet connection, a professional firm, or a business that manufactures a product.

In most businesses, the critical factors will be sales and customers. At startup, how many customers/clients will you have? What is your plan for acquiring customers? How many customers do you need to keep your business alive and growing?

Struggling/Surviving Stage

This is the difficult stage. Many businesses never go beyond this stage. A good marketing plan, financial plan and strategic plan can make a huge difference here, because the planning processes cause owners to think through each of these areas. Some people start their business without a marketing plan because they are convinced their product is so good it will sell itself. That seldom happens.

There is a popular expression among startup companies—"Fail fast!" This isn't intended to encourage anyone to fail, but to recognize failure as early as possible and get out quick. A small business owner who recognizes that for any reason the business is unlikely to succeed and sells or closes, is then in a position to consider a new venture. Staying with a dying business can deplete your assets as well as your physical and emotional resources, interfering with your ability to move forward with your life.

Obviously, a lot of businesses survive this stage and go on to thrive, and that is the incentive to start a business in the first place!

Growth Stage

When demand for your products exceeds what you can supply, you have two obvious choices— expand the supply or limit the demand.

Growth is the easy answer to increasing the supply of goods or services, and that may include adding people or equipment at your present location, moving to a better (larger) location, or expanding into multiple locations.

To reduce the demand, you may simply raise your prices, which in turn should increase your cash flow and your supply of capital. This is an easy and common solution wherever services are offered for periods of time. The obvious risk is that if you raise prices too much, your customers/clients may take their business elsewhere!

For a manufacturing business, growth may require a larger building, advanced or automated equipment, and more employees, while a retail business may consider a larger building or simply add branches (possibly by franchising).

In short, growth of a small business may be sudden (exploding out of the family garage and into a real manufacturing facility) or slow and deliberate, but in either case may take your business out of the "small" category into the larger world of business. Is your business a local, regional, national, or international operation? Has the business grown as large as it is likely to grow, or do you still have plans to keep expanding your markets? What will you need in order to continue your growth?

Maturity Stage

The business is established and stable. In this stage, your business may still be growing, but you have qualified, responsible staff or managers in every position. Your business may stay in this stage for a long time.

Decline Stage

Not all businesses go through this stage.

Hardly anyone expects their business to decline, but it happens, often through no fault of the owners. In 1981, businesses of all sizes, around the world had typewriters, which produced most of the business documents, from letters to invoices. That year, IBM introduced a personal computer that included word processing and spreadsheet software.

Ten years later, the typewriter industry had virtually disappeared. Nothing the owners or managers could have done would have saved those businesses. Ironically, IBM, who introduced the personal computer, had left the typewriter business as well.

Exit Stage

How do you leave a business that you worked for years to build—where you know every person in the company and so many people who have been a part of this adventure?

First, it's best to get rid of the emotion. Whether someone has offered to buy you out, or you're thinking about listing the business with a broker, park the emotion and sit down with your accountant. Decide what the business is really worth, or talk to a business broker and get an assessment.

Are you really ready to sell? Yes? Then this is the place to ask yourself a series of valuable questions, famously introduced to journalism students, often in their first class. Very appropriate here, and sometimes known as the 5 Ws and an H (Who, What, When, Where, Why, and How).

- Who? Who could, would, or should buy, inherit, or take over your business?
- What? What should trigger your exit decision? What will you have to offer a buyer?
- When? When would you like to exit? Which stage? What time in your life?

Change the thinking: When *should* you exit? As mentioned earlier, "Fail fast" suggests that as soon as you see your new business is not gaining traction, close it! Don't pour good money after bad. Move on to a better opportunity, or at least save your capital for a better idea.

- Where? Where will you go when you exit? Retire, start another business, look for work?
- Why? Why do you want to exit the business? Bank the profits? Tired? Need to escape from a difficult situation? Retire? Health? Simply because you can?
- How? How will this exit be managed? Cash? Stock? Notes? Close the business?

Many young businesses are started with an idea or product that the owners believe will lead to substantial growth and value. Their long term plan is simple— grow the business until it can be sold at a high price, either in a public stock offering or to a substantial buyer.

A personal experience

I had at times thought my children, or possibly my grandchildren would take over my export business. Frankly, they were not interested. I discussed a sale with one of my key customers, but

---

> when I was ready to exit, they were not prepared, so I simply retired. My business was based on personal relationships and a great deal of trust, both with suppliers and with buyers. That, combined with the fact that I had operated the business through most of its existence as a one-person (plus computer) enterprise meant that there was no real structure and no experienced staff to carry on. For me, this was the best exit, however, for most small business owners, a better exit strategy may prove more profitable.

Any business stage that you have not yet experienced is part of your future. Which stage is your business in now? What is the next stage, and what do you have to achieve to move into that stage? What changes or impacts do you anticipate when you move to the next stage? Understanding the business stages helps you prepare for those changes and their resulting impacts.

Tipping Points

Studying the future is largely about anticipating change. Not long after I earned my degree as a futurist, Malcolm Gladwell published a book, *The Tipping Point*. Many futurists were captivated by the concept, adopting tipping points as a new tool for anticipating or explaining change.

What do tipping points have to do with small business? The reason for introducing them here is to ask the question, "How (or when) does a business move from one stage to the next?"

With some transitions, the change is obvious. When you start spending money to create your business, when you negotiate the first sale, or open the doors to your business, you are clearly in the

Startup stage. Your enthusiasm may carry you through to the Struggling stage, but where is the line, or the tipping point that moves you from one stage to the next? It may come the day your bookkeeper announces that you made a profit—three months in a row! That could be sufficient to move you into the Growth stage.

The point is that tipping points don't announce themselves, but a tipping point is a change of direction, and a change of direction will probably impact the future.

You will probably recognize one after you pass it, or you can make your own definition for success. You can decide in advance how you will define the change from one business stage to the next. You can define success—or failure— and you can make decisions in advance as to when and how you will respond to passing each tipping point.

Tipping points can very well be a part of change between the stages of business growth, because there is a time when one stage loses strength to the next stage, and where the new stage starts taking over.

Business Models

Business models and value propositions are not methods of foresight, but they are components of the future for your business. Your business model describes what your business does and how it earns income and makes a profit. Also very important is a "Customer Value Proposition." What does your customer receive (product or service), and what is the value of that product or service to the customer?

Traditionally, business models fall into four basic categories:

- A *creator* could be an inventor or designer who sells or rents rights to use copyrights or patents, a miner that sells raw

44

materials, a game or application designer or a manufacturer that makes and sells finished products.

- *Distributors* buy products and resell them in the same form to others.

- *Landlords* sell the *temporary* right to use an asset such as a building, a car, a hotel room, a domain name, web site hosting, or an airline seat. Contractors and consultants are classified as landlords who sell services produced by humans.

- *Brokers* bring buyers and sellers together for a fee or commission.

Today, business models are changing. Technology has introduced new models and new approaches to defining business models. Artificial intelligence, which may become a new model in its own right, is spawning new models. Shaping Tomorrow (www.shapingtomorrow.com), for example, has a resident robot named Athena who searches for trends and changes throughout the world. Athena recently searched through nearly 2000 online articles to identify trends and change in business models. In the report, Athena suggested that "the top areas of emerging business model change will be in networking, media and entertainment, advertising, 3D printing, blockchain, tax, medicine and buildings."

In short, the world is changing. Personal computers created the opportunity and the need for the Internet. Technology and infrastructure costs created opportunities for mobile or cellular phones. The Internet created the opportunity and need for search engines and social networking, each of which have created more opportunities, more demand and more needs.

All part of change.

Change is happening faster, and more opportunities are opening up for new and small businesses. The forces of technology that allowed me to do business around the world with only a computer and a small space at home in the late twentieth century will allow more and more individuals to start business with only experience and technology as their partners. I suspect that in the next decade or two, a one-person business with no employees will produce the first individual unicorn—a one-billion-dollar business owned by one-person and operated with no employees. Artificial intelligence will make that possible.

Your Value Proposition

Why should anyone buy whatever products or services you are offering?

Is your product or service new, unique, fashionable, or useful? Does it fill a need or solve a problem? Do you have a price, quality, or fashion advantage? What does your product or service do for the buyer that justifies the cost?

Your value proposition will impact the future of your business. It will help you justify the price of your product or service, but you will have to convince potential buyers of that value.

In the next chapter you will consider the people and organizations who have a stake in the future of your business.

CHAPTER 3

Stakeholders in Your Business

Concept

What, or who, is a stakeholder and why should you be interested or concerned? Futurists use the term stakeholder to describe people or organizations that have a personal or financial interest in your business. That could include owners, investors, lenders, employees, suppliers, landlords, and customers. At the same time, you as a business owner are a stakeholder, and should be aware of your interests, risks and benefits.

Stakeholders

Your business will be influenced by people and organizations who have an interest in your business— your stakeholders. In turn, your business will affect the lives of family members, employees, customers, suppliers and other businesses, who also have a stake in the future of your business. Who are the stakeholders in your business, now and in the future?

A stakeholder may be an individual or organization that could

1) impact your business or

2) be impacted by your business.

Customers and suppliers are examples of individuals or organizations whose actions may affect your business. For example, a customer may impact your business by substantially increasing or decreasing the amount of their purchases. The higher the percentage of your sales to that customer, the greater the impact. The same logic applies to suppliers.

Partners, close business associates, and their spouses can have very strong influences and impacts on your business and your future, both positive and negative.

It can be valuable to know your stakeholders and understand their interests, their personalities, and their values. Be aware of their strengths and weaknesses. Know what they can do *for* you or what they could do *to* you. Know them as well as you would know a marriage partner, because they are, or can be, important to the future of your business.

Here's a short list of examples:

Examples- Stakeholders interest in your business

Stakeholders	What is the interest of this stakeholder in your business?
Employees	Careers, jobs, compensation.
Customers/Clients	Value and quality of the products and services offered by your business.
Suppliers (including landlord)	Continuation of your reliance on suppliers to provide goods and services and pay bills in a timely manner.
Local and national governments	Collect taxes, build infrastructure, protect citizens, create and enforce laws.
Banker	Maintain accounts, monitor financial status, possible lender.

Figure 3.1- Examples of people and organizations that have a stakeholder interest in your business.

Which relationships are critical to the future of your business?

If you have a single customer that provides most of your income, what are the risks? If that customer does not pay promptly, what is the impact? What if that customer switches to another supplier or goes out of business?

Similarly, are you dependent in any way on a single supplier? What would be the impact on your business if that supplier went out of business or lost the ability to provide a critical product?

A personal experience

In the building next door to my small business, a candle manufacturing business took an order from a division of Hallmark, the greeting card company, for several truckloads of candles. Described as "tiny tapers" they were long and slim, with a base of ¼ inch. A very large order for the candle company with a potential to change their future.

I learned about this while having coffee with the manager of the candle company. When the trucks arrived at Hallmark, ALL of the candles were rejected because they did not meet the size specifications. In short, the candle company did not have a quality control system, and they now faced huge losses.

I asked Darrel if Hallmark would still allow him to fill the order for the tiny tapers, and he said "Yes, if the tapers meet their quality control specs." At the end of the morning, I had become the quality control department for the candle company, working under an excellent contract to sort all the returned candles and repackage the tapers that met specs as well as the replacement candles. Within a week I had hired a crew to sort candles, created gauges to check the minimum and maximum diameters of each candle, and mounted the gauges on sorting tables. By the time the four trailer loads had been sorted and re-shipped to Hallmark (where they were accepted), my crew was handling *all* quality control and packaging for the candle company.

Several months later, an East Coast firm offered to buy the candle company, and on 48 hours' notice my contract was terminated. The candle company had risked their business on one large order to a large potential customer. I temporarily expanded my young business around the needs of one company, growing quickly, then ending suddenly.

I cannot claim wisdom or analysis, but I was aware from the beginning that the relationship with the candle company could end quickly, so I did not invest on their behalf. I supplied only labor, training, and experience. Any investments in equipment, materials, space, or utilities were provided by the candle company, so my risk was minimal. The benefit to my small company was simple, we expanded our cash position substantially, with very little risk.

For each stakeholder in your business, ask yourself— what is your relationship now, and what elements of that relationship could change over the next ten years.

How will changes in your business over the next ten years impact your stakeholders, including employees and customers? Will present employees be able to grow into new roles as the business grows? Will some retire or leave for other reasons?

Obviously, stakeholders represent only one relationship between your business and the future, but it's an important place to start thinking about the future.

Who will your business affect or impact?

At the same time that you are looking at stakeholders in your business, it is important to recognize that you are also a stakeholder, with needs and interests to be served.

You are a Stakeholder

Businesses, groups or individuals in which your business has a stakeholder interest	What is your interest in this individual, group, or business?
Managers and employees	Honesty, capability, reliability, long term relationship.
Suppliers	Reliable source long term, good quality, fair price.
Customers	Continuing relationship and timely payment.
Landlord	Sound facility, reliable access, affordable.
Financial services and lenders	Consistent service and fair terms.
Governments	Fair, impartial government, law enforcement, infrastructure, legal system at all levels.

Figure 3.2- You are also a stakeholder. What do you seek in your relationships, now and in the future?

Again, look at this list with an eye to the future and how any of these relationships might change, for better or worse, over the next ten years.

Although stakeholder analysis is helpful, and can be valuable, too much negative focus on relationship risks can lead to distrust of everyone! Too much trust also has risks, so a balanced view of relationships is important. Your suppliers, customers, partners and employees are valuable to your business. Some businesses have found it useful to include key stakeholders in their strategic planning process, sharing and preparing plans for growth together in the future.

CHAPTER 4

Forces and Trends: Anticipating Change

Concept

The future is about change, because change is what makes the future different from the present. Change in your life and in your business is brought about by forces, the forces that exist in your life, in your business and in the world around you.

What Is a Force?

You cannot see a force. When the wind blows, you can see the leaves flutter and the branches bend. You can even feel the wind, but you cannot *see* the wind. The same is true of gravity— we can see the effects of gravity, when things fall down, but we cannot see gravity.

In your life and in your business, there are forces that you can identify and see the impacts without seeing the force itself. In this chapter we will focus on internal forces— the forces *inside* your business. In doing so, we will divide your business into six categories of forces, all with common names, and each composed of multiple forces within each category.

Large organizations tend to focus their long term and strategic planning on large, external forces, including Social, Technological, Economic, Ecologic and Political forces. Small businesses must focus more on internal forces, the forces that are driving change from within the business, as discussed below.

Domains

A domain is a category of internal forces. "Finances" for example. The category "finances" contains several different forces (cash, payables, receivables, taxes, etc.), and any one of these forces may be a dominant or driving force over a period of time. Cash may be a driving force when there is either too little or too much of it. Taxes may be a driving force when you have a problem with your taxes. Below are six domains that are common to small businesses.

Six Domains of a Small Business

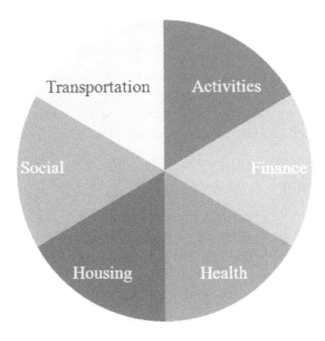

Figure 4.1- Your business in six parts, the six domains of internal forces.

Internal domains are made up of the forces and sub-forces that are a direct part of your business. These are forces that impact your business and with which you must interact. When these forces pressure you or motivate you, they are called *driving* forces. Here, we recognize six categories of forces that are common to all businesses and are a part of each small or medium sized business throughout the firm's existence.

Finances

Everything to do with money in your business. This includes cash, receivables, payables, cash flow, assets, debt, taxes, insurance and accounting.

Location

Wherever and everywhere your business is located. This domain includes land, buildings, parking areas, traffic count, zoning, city, country and access to facilities such as water, utilities, freeways and port areas.

Operations

The production of goods and services, including quality control, reports, tools, equipment, processes, inventories, and logistics required to move raw materials in and finished goods out.

Management

The leadership that provides direction and accountability for the organization.

Marketing

The portion of the organization that is devoted to promoting and selling the products or services provided by the business.

People

All the people in, and directly related to the business: owners, managers, staff, suppliers, advisors, contractors.

In short, your business can be divided into six domains, six groups of forces that will exert themselves in support of, and sometimes in conflict with, the other domains. These areas of your business are the forces you must manage, balance, and anticipate as you take your business into the future.

If you are in a one-person business, you may be looking at these domains thinking that they don't work for you because you are the only person in your business. That's the point—these domains exist in every business, and sooner or later you will have to deal with all of them.

Now, let's take a deeper look at these domains.

1. **Finances-** The Finance domain includes everything related to finances. For example: capital, cash flow, income, assets, expense, debt, liabilities, financial risks, taxes, insurance, and accounting are all forces within this domain.

   If your business at some point has inadequate cash flow, you may be forced to take some kind of action in order to make payroll, pay bills and meet your financial obligations. You may have to aggressively collect money from customers, negotiate a loan or sell an asset in order to raise sufficient cash.

   To meet the requirements of local and national governments to pay taxes, you are required to account for all funds that you collect or pay out, as well as pay those taxes in a timely manner.

   If your business generates more money than is required for operations, you may choose to pay amounts to yourself and partners, create reserve accounts for future expansions or acquisitions, or invest to create more income.

2. **Location-** The Location domain includes the building(s) you occupy and all related facilities such as parking, loading and storage areas. Your business may be required to be located in specific zones, such as industrial, commercial, office, retail and other areas zoned for categories of businesses.

You may choose to locate in areas that have high pedestrian traffic (retail store) near parks (apartment building), large parking areas (office building) a good view (restaurant) or an industrial zone (manufacturing).

3. **Operations-** The Operations domain focuses on the areas where your products or services are produced or created. This may include the purchasing and receiving of raw materials, parts and supplies, inventories and the logistics for moving materials in and finished goods out.

   In professional organizations, operations may be conducted in offices, client areas, and examination rooms. Operations for a restaurant or retail store might include the entire location, while many small businesses produce their services on computers, which may be located in a room in one's home or in office buildings.

4. **Management-** The Management domain provides organization, administration, and leadership to the business.

   Management selects the legal structure, is responsible for compliance with all applicable laws, and defines the core business and any divisions of the organization.

   Management is responsible for the entire organization.

5. **Marketing-** The Marketing domain is responsible for the public image of the business (publicity, promotion, advertising) and all its products or services. In addition, Marketing is responsible for sales of products and services and for customer/client satisfaction.

6. **People-** The People domain embraces all the individuals inside the business as well as those outside the organization that have regular contact with or influence the business. This includes owners, staff, suppliers, advisors, contractors, and customers.

Forces within each Domain

Domains	Common forces or sub-domains
Finances	Accounting Receivables, credit Payables, debt Cash flow Taxes
Location	Building Utilities Traffic Parking Community (Physical) Maintenance
Operations	Raw materials Assembly Quality control Packaging Shipping/delivery
Management	Growth Quality New products or services Investment Planning Risk, insurance
Marketing	Sales Distribution Design Advertising Publicity Social media

Figure 4.2- Each of the business domains can be divided into forces, or sub-domains. The sub-domains may vary with industries, practices, and individual businesses.

What Is a Trend?

Futurists and the media talk about trends a lot. But what are these trends, and what do they mean to you?

The reason people are interested in the future is that they want to know what will change. Trends indicate change, and change is what makes the future different from the present.

Most of the trends that you will hear about in the media and from futurists are the big-picture trends, and they generally fall into five categories: social change, technological change, economics, ecology, and politics. Understanding these trends is important as they will affect the world you live and work in. You will explore those external trends and forces in a later chapter. In this chapter, you will focus on the trends and forces inside your business: the *internal* forces.

A trend is an indicator of change and of the direction in which a change force is moving. A trend line is an image, usually a line derived from time-series data such as population statistics over a period of years. The line shows the direction a force is moving and whether the speed of the force is increasing or decreasing.

The chart below is an example of time-series data, and is a projection of the number of centenarians in the United States from 2000 through 2050. The time period is from 2000 to 2050, the series is in ten year intervals, and the data are the number of centenarians at each interval. The trend in this graph is upward, showing increasing numbers of centenarians each decade.

Time series data

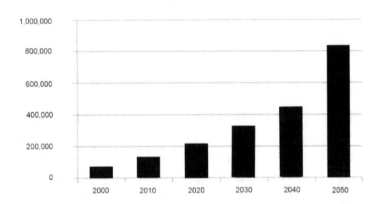

Figure 4.3- An example of time-series data. This is a projection of the number of centenarians in the United States from 2000 to 2050.

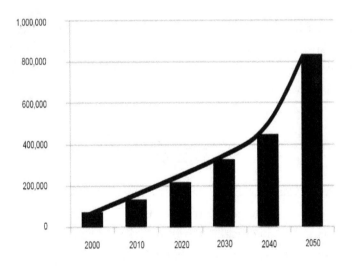

Figure 4.4 - The same data as figure 4.3, but with a trend line added. The angle of the trend line indicates the speed of change.

A trend line is a picture (or a drawing) representing change in data over a period of time. Once you have a trend line showing the change from the past to the present, you can start thinking about the future of that trend. Where will the trend line go next? Will it go up or down? Why?

If you are familiar with the data that lie under the trend line, you can probably make some pretty good guesses about the direction of the trend line over the next year or two. But the farther into the future you look, the more uncertain the future is likely to become. The possibilities for change become greater as you move further away from the present.

Whenever you are looking at a trend line or extending a trend line into the future, it is valuable to keep asking, "What could cause the line to change direction? Or not?"

In most cases, straight lines oversimplify the image of change, but human aging is one example of a true linear trend. Every day, every week, every year, everyone gets a little older. Unlike other forces, aging is constant.

Megatrends

John Naisbitt wrote the book "Megatrends" in 1984. It sold over nine million copies and introduced much of the world to the forces of change— specifically, ten trends that were changing the world. Generally, these forces of change would take decades to unfold, would have global impacts, and would transform societies.

Climate change is an example of a megatrend (not included in Naisbitt's book). Global warming has been a concern for decades, but the concept has been ridiculed by people, organizations, and industries (the coal industry, for example) that would be impacted by efforts to mitigate global warming. Industries that would benefit (solar power and wind power, for examples) trumpet the urgency and benefits of reducing global warming.

In short, major change of any kind will have positive and negative impacts. IBM, for example recognized the trend toward personal computers, introducing the IBM PC in 1981. Five years later, IBM discontinued production of their very popular "Selectric" typewriter, which had become a victim of the rise of personal computers.

The impacts of robotics, artificial intelligence, DNA research, the rise of China and other major trends are the source of considerable speculation today, and will almost certainly have influence on your business in the years to come.

Possible, Plausible and Probable

Anything is possible, but …

Futurists have to give considerable thought to possible, plausible, and probable events that may occur in the future. How do you sort these out or even try to define them? Below is a simple diagram that will help to clarify the differences.

The large outer oval represents everything that can possibly happen in your business. If you apply this diagram to your business and future, this "Possible" circle contains all of the events that could possibly happen in the future. This includes high-probability events, low-probability events, and everything in between. Possible, Plausible, and Probable.

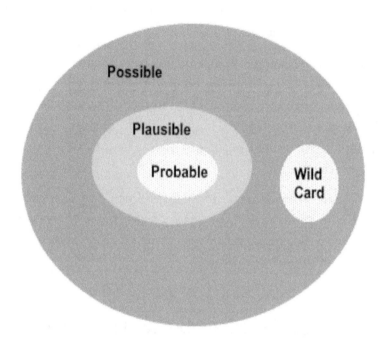

Figure 4.5- A diagram showing the relationships between possible, plausible, probable, and wild card futures and events. You will use these concepts of possible, plausible, probable, and wild cards throughout this book

The next smaller oval is labeled "Plausible". Within this oval are the events that have a reasonable chance of happening in the future. Some plausible events will actually happen and others may not, but they are plausible. For example, complete failure of your business, wild success of your business, losing money, or an employee being injured on the job may all be unlikely in your business, they are all possible and plausible events.

Inside the plausible area is one more oval, labeled "Probable." Within this oval are the events that will probably happen in your business. Events that could happen might include installing a new computer system, hiring an employee or contractor, borrowing money, creating or updating a business plan, marketing plan, or strategic plan, creating or updating a web site, developing a new product or service, acquiring or losing an important customer or client.

The probable circle contains the events that you should be aware of and for which you should be planning, particularly those events that will have a strong impact on your business. Some events are highly probable, like license renewals, and tax filings, but they do not have much impact on your business (unless you forget them). As you will see in later chapters, *strategic planning will focus on the events that have both a high probability of occurring and will have a strong impact on your business.*

The wild card circle is by itself. Events in this circle are neither plausible nor probable. Wild card events are low-probability, high-impact events like a flood, fire, earthquake, hurricane or other natural events, and are not likely to occur. But could!

You will have a chance to look at wild card events in some detail in Section 2 on developing scenarios. In addition, some low-probability, high-impact events will be included in the contingency plan for your business, which you will create later.

This chapter has focused on defining or clarifying terms or concepts so that you will be able to use these terms easily throughout the book. In the next chapter, you will examine trends and forces in your business and will learn how to extend trend lines into the future.

CHAPTER 5

Forces in Your Business: Past, Present, and Future

Concept

Forces of change that are likely to affect your business can be understood, anticipated, and altered. Once you understand what forces exist in your business, you will be able to recognize where those forces have been in the past, where they are now, and which plausible directions they may take in the future. It is a core concept among futurists that actions taken in the present can impact or change the directions of forces, resulting in changes in the future.

N ow that you know about the forces that impact your business, what can you do with them? How do you use that knowledge to see where the forces are going?

The answer is simple. Follow the forces that are in your business now and extend them into the future.

Futurists use trend lines to visualize the effects and impacts of different forces over time. They gather statistics about a force or its effects and draw a trend line. The trend line indicates the amount, direction, and speed of change up to the present. The futurist then tries to determine where the trend will go in the future. The trend may turn upward, it may continue to follow its present trajectory, or it may turn downward. The speed of change may slow or accelerate. Trend lines illustrate all of these changes.

One method of extending trend lines into the future is extrapolation. In extrapolating from a trend line, a common approach is to extend two lines from the present into the future. They include a positive or best plausible projection and a negative or worst plausible projection.

How do you apply those tools to better understand the future of your business?

This chapter is about: visualizing the past, present, and future of your business.

Visualizing the domains in your business

How do you see the changes in your business, whether in the past, present, or future? One answer is to create your own trend lines. As mentioned earlier, trend lines are usually based on statistics, or measurements. That means that you will have to capture statistical information for your business and turn those statistics into graphs that will show change in your business. That may sound complex, but you are probably already generating this information in your bookkeeping system, whether you are using a spreadsheet, software like QuickBooks, or an accounting firm.

How do you measure change in your business? That is the problem I came up against when I was trying to apply futures methods to my own small business. What should I measure?

First, I concluded that measuring "business" was too general. I had already identified the six domains, so that was a logical place to start. Measure the domains, or specifically the components of the domains that indicate change. For example:

SMALL BUSINESS FORESIGHT

- Finances
    - Sales
    - Expenses
    - Profit/Loss
- Location
    - Rent or depreciation
    - Maintenance
    - Taxes
    - Utilities
- Operations
    - Numbers of products produced
    - Numbers of services produced
    - Costs of production
- Management
    - Costs of management
        - Salaries
        - Expenses
        - Consulting fees
- Marketing
    - Marketing expense
        - Payroll
        - Advertising
        - Printing
        - Promotion
    - Sales
        - Products and services
        - In person
        - On line
        - Store or office
- People
    - Number of people
    - Total payroll

71

At first glance, this looks like a lot of work to get some statistics. In reality, your bookkeeping software probably produces graphs (and pie charts) for all these areas. Once you get the information, you can decide which items are most important to you and look at those monthly. You may follow slow-changing items quarterly. In either case, remember that you are looking for change—the amount and the direction of change.

How do you create financial statistics if you haven't started your business, or if it is still very new? Look at your business plan, your anticipated profit and loss statement, and your marketing plan. Each of these forecasts anticipate income and expense, and you can use those numbers to help develop scenarios about the future for your business.

In your business, you may find other areas that you consider to be specific indicators of change that are important to you, such as backorders from suppliers. Add them in and monitor them.

A Trend Line

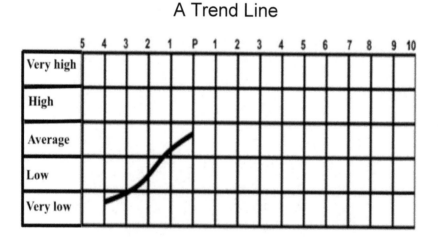

Figure 5.1 - An example of a trend line in a graph. This line shows how one business has changed in one domain over the four years

since startup to the present (P). The header starts at (5) years in the past, goes to (P), Present, and to ten years in the future.

Once you start creating your own trend lines, what do you look for? Primarily, you will be looking for change, particularly in the past few years. Is the trend line moving up, down, or staying level? How fast is the line changing? Are things getting better or worse? Figure 5.1 shows a trend line that has risen since the business was formed four years ago. Notice that in the second and third year after the business started, the line rises faster. The speed of change has accelerated.

One of the advantages of creating trend lines for each domain is that you will recognize change more quickly within the narrow focus of one domain than you may see over the broader focus of your entire business. By looking at six different parts of your business separately, you will be able to recognize which parts of your business are changing and whether those changes are positive or negative. Once you recognize what is changing, you will be able to make decisions or develop strategies to improve your business and your future.

How do you make a trend line?

In a blank chart like the one below, simply select the quality level (Very low to Very high) during each year of the business' existence. Here is a point where your *Small Business Foresight Workbook* will be helpful (http://www.smallbusinessforesight.com), as there are blank charts in the workbook that will help you create your graphs.

The basic form is:

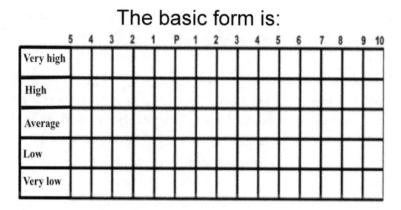

Figure 5.2 – A blank graph format for plotting the quality of change in your business from five years in the past to the present (P), with space to project up to ten years into the future.

Each of these blank graphs is designed for you to draw a line that expresses your opinion about the quality of change in that domain over the past five years. Obviously, this graph is not designed for precision, and precision is not expected or desired. You can accomplish all this on any piece of paper, even on the back of an envelope. This is simply a way for you to draw a picture (line) of how you feel about the quality of change in each domain over the past five years. That line will be a base, a launching point into the future. If you are not comfortable with the generic headings in these examples, change them! Make the charts fit your business.

In my workshops, this is the point where someone asks, "How do I mark the square?" The answer is, "Any way you want to." Some people make an X, some draw a line. They are all right. Whatever looks right to you will be fine.

When you have marked each column up to the present, draw a line from the first mark to the second and on through each mark. Once you have drawn your line (this is a trend line) in each domain

74

representing your business up to the present, you will have a foundation for projecting into the future for each domain.

Looking Into the Future

Now that you can visualize the directions of the forces at work at the present, you are ready to look into the future. This involves extending the trend lines in each of your domains ten years into the future. For each domain, you will draw two lines into the future. One line will represent the *best plausible* future for that domain, and the second will represent the *worst plausible* future for that domain.

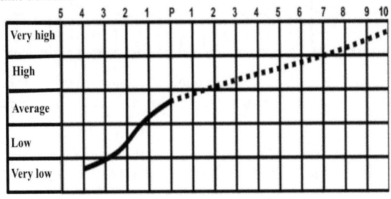

Figure 5.3 - A trend line extended to show the best plausible potential futures for the next ten years.

Before you start drawing, ask yourself what events in the future could cause the upper line to rise. Increasing sales might cause this line to rise. On the other hand, what might cause the lower line to fall in the chart below? Extreme competition or new technology?

The Cone of Uncertainty

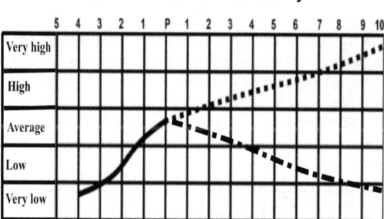

Figure 5.4- A 10 year projection into the future. Notice that the two lines diverge to form a cone, commonly known as "the cone of uncertainty."

Notice that the two lines projecting into the future form a cone. That is because the lines extending into the future are going into the unknown. As you travel away from the present into the future, the uncertainty increases, so the lines spread farther apart because more plausible events can occur as the future becomes more uncertain. Futurists call the area between the two lines the "cone of uncertainty." This area is important because the lines you have created form boundaries on plausible futures for your business.

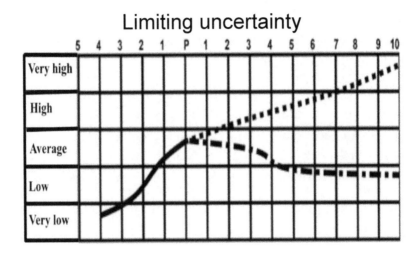

Figure 5.5- Notice that the bottom line flattens out in the "Low" range. This is because the owners have determined that if the business falls below that point they will close the business, removing some uncertainty and risk.

Think about your business right now. Unless you are at a big transition point, you probably know what your business will be doing for the next year or two. Three to five years will raise some uncertainties, and the possibilities for change or surprises keep increasing every year. That explains why the two lines tend to spread apart as they go farther away from the present and into the future.

In the graph above, assuming the Marketing domain, this business started four years ago and grew slowly the first year, a little faster the second, and accelerated in the third and fourth years. The owners believe that if everything goes well the business will continue to expand steadily over the next ten years.

The lower line anticipates the possibility of competition developing with improved products or services, as well as the impact of an economic downturn in the second or third year. The owners believe that if the business falls below average, they will either sell the business or close the doors rather than risk losses.

This illustrates that you can reflect many possibilities in your charts, both positive and negative.

Your projections probably will not look like the classic cone of uncertainty because you have divided your business into six parts. Looking at your business in sections encourages you to think specifically about each part of your business, narrowing your focus on the future. In addition, you are encouraged to insert specific knowledge about the apparent or plausible risks that exist that might impact the future for your business.

Plausible and Possible Futures

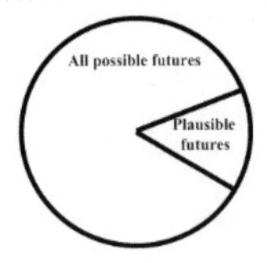

Figure 5.6- The circle represents all possible futures over any period of time. The wedge offers a different view of the "cone of uncertainty" and represents the plausible futures over the same time period.

Wild cards

Futurists define wild cards as low-probability, high-impact events. Wild card events occur in the areas outside the cone of plausibility and can be either positive or negative.

As you can see, this diagram represents "All possible futures". By putting boundaries on the *plausible* futures, we have narrowed the area of the future that you need to explore.

What about the rest of the circle in Figure 5.6, the implausible futures? These are the futures that are not likely to happen, but could occur because they are possible—like winning the lottery.

Futurists define wild cards as low-probability, high-impact events. Wild card events occur in the areas outside the cone of plausibility and can be either positive or negative. Wild cards will be discussed in detail in Chapter 7, "Events that will Impact or Change Your Business".

Projecting into the future

The six domains within your business are segments of your total business, so you may be aware of specific risks or opportunities that may occur in any one of these domains. For example, you may expect a technological advance that could revolutionize your industry. Or, you may anticipate new technology that would make your business obsolete. The point is that your trend lines don't have to be straight lines or even gentle curves. They can reflect known, plausible risks or opportunities.

The emphasis here is on *plausible*. Consider the positive events that could reasonably occur over the next ten years in each domain. You are expected to be optimistic, but keep your projections within the plausible range. What could happen in a domain that would improve the quality or success of your business and cause the upper line to rise higher? Or what would keep it from rising? Keep asking yourself, "What are the best things I can *reasonably* expect to happen in this domain?"

Then look at plausible negative events. What negative, but plausible events could occur over the next ten years? A downturn in the business cycle? Unexpected competition? New technology that reduces demand for your products or services? What could cause the lower line in Figure 5.4 to drop more quickly?

Dominant Forces

Throughout the life of your business, one or two of the six domains discussed in Chapter 4 will be dominant—be a driving force—during any time period. These dominant domains may change from one stage of business development to the next. Moreover, the forces within a domain may change in importance. The question you will want to answer at the end of the chapter is: "Which of the six domains are likely to dominate the future of your business over the next ten years?"

The reason for this question is that in Step Two of the futuring process, you will explore alternate futures by constructing scenarios, and the driving forces in your business will determine the directions of the scenarios.

Which domains are dominant in your business now? Think about each of the six domains and ask yourself which domain is demanding your attention and time *right now*. When you have to make choices, which domain wins? For most business, the dominant domains are the Finances (cash flow) domain and the Marketing (sales) domain, but there are times when any one of the domains can become more important or have the greatest impact on your business.

Sometimes, activities in one domain may capture everyone's attention over a substantial period of time, with the risk of distracting from the domains that drive the business. For example, if the business is going to move to a new facility in the future, it is possible for the planning, preparation, and move to seriously disrupt the sales and production areas. Recognizing this risk in advance allows management to plan for a smooth transition and lessened impact.

The important thing here is that you think about and recognize the forces and domains that are influencing your business, now and each year in the future.

In this chapter we have focused on forces and domains because that is where decisions you make help to determine the future. In the next chapter, you will look at the big-picture forces, the forces in the world around you that may also shape your business and the future.

CHAPTER 6

Forces That Shape *Your* Worlds:

Global, National, and Local

Concept

Large organizations tend to focus on external forces, the forces over which small businesses have little direct control, but for which you must prepare. The forces that drive change in the world around you can be anticipated and understood. Understanding and being aware of these forces and how they might impact your business provides an opportunity to develop strategies for dealing with those impacts, whether positive or negative.

Awareness of changes in your community and the national economy as well as changing social or technological trends in the world around you should be built into your strategies and Action Plans. This can translate into simple awareness – for example, in your community, be aware of planned future projects that might affect your business or your property, positively or negatively. Be aware of movements or activity to create laws or regulations that may impact you.

How do you deal with the forces that you cannot influence or control? Futurists find the answer to that question in one word:

Anticipation

If you anticipate what may happen in the world around you, you can prepare. You can take a defensive position and minimize the impacts or damage, much as you might prepare for a hurricane or other natural disaster. You can also take an offensive or proactive position, profiting from the big changes that occur in the world.

In 2008, not everyone suffered financial losses when the world economy turned downward. Some individuals and organizations anticipated the downturn and withdrew from financial positions, sold expensive homes, sold stocks, and made other moves to reduce exposure to losses. When the financial markets collapsed, those people did not suffer big losses. Some took positive action and reinvested in low-priced assets and experienced gains as the market returned toward normal.

Anticipating change is valuable in understanding the future. Anticipation allows you to avoid surprises, or at least reduces the number of high-impact surprises. Anticipation allows you to prepare for the future.

STEEP

Many futurists use the mnemonic "STEEP" to remind businesses of some of the outside forces that may affect or impact them.

Social forces

Technological forces

Economic forces

Ecologic forces

Political forces

These categories are usually thought of in terms of big change (in the world or a country), but they apply all the way down to your community, so you should be aware of these types of change and how, or if, they will impact you.

Social change may be on either a global or very local scale. A country emerging from poverty, a growing religious movement, protest movements, revolution, immigration, increased education, and equality for minorities are all examples. The Internet has changed the way the world communicates, offering instant communication in written, voice and video formats. It also allows individuals to find individuals or groups with similar interests. In your community, you may see social change as schools teach immigrant children the language of their new country, or as you communicate with people around the world whom you have never met.

Somewhere between social change and technological change lies a generation of people born since 1990 who are digital natives. They have grown up with digital beeps, digital clocks, calculators, cell phones, computers, and all the other digital devices that are normal in our world today.

Technological change may be the most obvious area of change as you watch the continuing evolution of the Internet, new medical advances, space exploration, telephones that have become computers, robots in your business (and in your vehicles) as technologies become smarter and new research advances many fields rapidly. The technology in your own home as well as in your business is probably changing to make you more aware of the world around you, providing information about nearly everything.

Your doctor has rapidly improving diagnostic equipment; your community has increased surveillance tools to deter crime, and you can call people around the world individually or in groups with live video. Now, your cell phone can monitor your health, including your heart rate, heart rhythm, and body temperature and more as new apps appear. In some cases, a smart watch may collect data from your body and deliver that information to your cell phone and your doctor.

Economic change on a large scale may come in many forms, including gradual inflation or a crushing recession. At a local level, governments may borrow money to build facilities or improve the local image but may raise your taxes to pay off the debt. In your community, a change in zoning, a new school, or an improved street may increase the value of your property, but also increase your taxes. On a national or international level, disputes between countries may bring changes in tariffs that may impact your costs of materials or your markets.

Ecologic change in the form of global warming or trash in our waterways and oceans is a serious concern world-wide, yet ecology starts with individuals, homes, businesses, and communities. If your community allows a local industry to release pollution into the air or into local waters, that pollution not only contributes to the worldwide problems but may directly harm you or your family as well. Awareness or participation in local activities that reduce pollution or protect and restore the environment may have an impact on your life.

Political change is everywhere and constant, even when it is not apparent. Change is most obvious in countries and organizations that have open elections, but continues even in countries that attempt to stifle change. In the community where your business is located, understanding the political process and how it works can be very useful. Many communities have long-term, written plans in place, including plans to change or improve roads, annex adjacent properties, expand water and sewer systems, improve police and fire protection, and advance many other services. If you make the effort to learn what plans are pending or already in place, you will be better prepared to deal with their impacts.

Scanning Your Horizons

In the days of sailing ships, a sailor was frequently posted in the "crow's nest," a platform high on a mast with uninterrupted visibility looking ahead, behind and on all sides, or 360 degrees. The sailor scanned the horizon and reported whatever he saw— sails, land, whales, or storms—to the crew below.

Futurists use a method called environmental scanning, or horizon scanning, which amounts to a conscious effort to watch for and be aware of change. Scanning is a very useful approach that alerts businesses and organizations to any change that may impact them. Scanning is one of the basic and most used tools in the futurist's tool box. This tool can help you in your business as well.

You may find information in newspapers, web sites, trade magazines, television, online newsgroups, and online searches— almost anywhere.

Scanning is simply a matter of paying attention, always asking yourself how any piece of information might impact your business now or in the future. One source for information on global trends is the Millennium Project web site at http://www.millennium-project.org. The section titled "15 Global Challenges" is updated annually by futurists from all parts of the world.

The news media are very aware of scanning and trends, so you will see frequent articles or stories in the news about new trends that are changing the future. Read, look, and listen; then make up your own mind about what is really happening or how any change might impact your business. You can get different viewpoints about nearly any potential trend on Google or a favorite search engine. As you read or listen, keep asking how this trend might affect your business. When someone tells you about impending change, dig deeper. Remember how you made trend lines for each domain, and ask yourself, "What is causing this change? Is there data, or is this someone's opinion?" And keep asking, "Why? What is causing this trend line to move up or down? What will be the impacts of this change?"

One important challenge related to scanning is "information overload"—more information than you can easily manage or keep track of. When I was at the University of Houston, students referred to the information overload as "trying to drink from a firehose".

Don't try to collect every article or piece of information about the future. Keep asking yourself if this piece of information will affect your business, and keep only what informs you. You are scanning for a reason, a purpose— to protect and advance your business. Scanning will provide a foundation for growing your business into the future. Scanning is valuable — it keeps you informed about the future, including

- Change in your world, country, community and industry.
- Recognize trends and forces of change
- Opportunities
- Threats
- Business cycle
- Competition
- Clients/customers

Now that you have information coming in, what do you do with it?

Organizing information—your scan hits

What do you do with the information you find in your scanning? One approach is to record the basic information about the source—title, date, publication so you can find that information again when you need the reference. Keep in mind that information stored on a web site is subject to change and may not be there when you need it.

Blank Scanning Worksheet

	World	National	Local
Social			
Technology			
Economic			
Ecologic			
Political			

Figure 6.1-- A blank worksheet from the *Small Business Foresight Workbook* that organizes scan hits by STEEP category and broad geography. As you start recording scan hits, you will become aware of what is important for you to save. At that point, revise your worksheet to meet your needs.

The simple layout in Figure 6.1 can be created in Excel or any spreadsheet software in your computer or on any sheet of paper to keep track of information you find that may impact the future of your business. The advantage of creating a table in word processing or spreadsheet software is that each section is expandable

Just as the six domains help you understand what is changing in your business world, the STEEP categories can help you understand what is happening in the world around you.

Following is a brief example of a STEEP Scanning Worksheet:

Example: Scanning Worksheet

Forces	World	National	Local
Social	Business Week 1/16/15 Forever pill Scientific American 10/14 Inclusion and Diversity 5 articles Sci American 12/14 The Gene Genie	Fast Co. 3/15- Prison reform Wired 2/15- Whole new world/Male birth control	WSJ 4/9/12 Retirement WSJ 12/21/13 Retirement Income Bloomberg1/12/15 Healthcare at the Mall
Tech-nology	Discover 3/15 Alzheimer's Brain-also Dr and Salamander regeneration Wired 9/14- AI Knows Your Mind	Inc 2/15- Cruise Control Fast Co 12/14 Cloud's Next Phase Sci American 8/14 Accidental Genius	Inc 11/14 internet of Things (your office) Bloomberg 1/19/15 Hydrogen Can Power Cars and Homes

	Sci American 12/14- Ten world Changing Ideas	Bloomberg 1/26/15 Solution to Antibiotic Resistance	
Economic	Bloomberg 12/29/14 Coal Begin to Cool in China Bloomberg 11/24/14 Cash is for Losers	Bloomberg12 /22/14 Drop in US Fertility Rate	Inc. 2/15 Launch for under $10,000 Inc. 12/14 The Exit Lab (for small biz owners)
Ecologic	Scientific American 2/15 Science 9/14 Global Strategy for Coastal Pops. Bloomberg 1/12/15 Water's Future		
Political	Bloomberg 1/26/15 India Arms Race with China	Sci American 11/14 Solar Wars	

Figure 6.2- A brief example of a STEEP Scanning Worksheet

Keep asking yourself, "What does this development (or change) mean to my business or to my customers or suppliers?" Is this a trend or something that could become a trend? How could that trend affect you or your business? Also, ask yourself those journalism questions—Who-What-When-Where-Why and How?

You have probably noticed that this worksheet puts a lot of emphasis on "Where?"— Local, National, or World? If you are doing business on the other side of the world, then international news can be important, especially if you are shipping to an area where the risks have just increased.

Also ask yourself how these news stories affect your customers and the markets you plan to serve. Do you see opportunities? Threats?

A Personal Experience

In the mid-1990s, I had shipped a 40 foot container load of paper to Karachi. My bank notified me that payment had not been received on time, and another day later I received a message from our agent. He apologized for the delay and said we should receive funds within a week, which we did. He went on to explain that the customer's bank had been bombed! He also suggested that my proposed visit to Karachi be postponed due to the ongoing violence. I agreed!

What about your suppliers? Do any of the articles you are reading suggest changes or impacts that might affect your suppliers, whether they are an ocean away, or very nearby? Will transportation be affected, and if so, how soon? What events might impact the cost or availability of the products you purchase? Threats of violence, political actions such as tariffs and trade wars are obvious, but what is the impact of the size of container ships? In the 1950s container ships carried up to 500 twenty foot container equivalents (TEU), or 250 40-foot containers. Today, large container ships can carry 15,000 TEUs, or 7500 forty-foot containers! Cargo companies work hard to fill those ships, and can be very competitive.

The advantage of foresight is that you can use all these details to anticipate changes in your costs and delivery times. Today, retailers are fine-tuning their plans for delivering types of goods to customers' homes with self-delivering vehicles—no drivers! Will that kind of technology be useful to you? Will you have to compete against it?

Think back ten, twenty or twenty-five years to see how quickly new technologies develop. Cell phones were very basic in the late 1990s—they made phone calls, but that was enough! In countries that had limited phone lines and facilities, customers had waited years to get a telephone installed in their home. Cell phones leapfrogged the two-wire system to homes and buildings, allowing people to get immediate phone service. It wasn't long before messaging and data became available.

Internet Explorer was introduced in 1995, just after Yahoo appeared. Google was introduced in 2004—the new, serious search engine. (I was doing research from 2000 to 2005, mostly from university libraries as the search engines and Internet providers were still limited).

What would be the impact on your business if Internet service or cell service was not available for a day, a week, or a month? How would that impact your business? What would you have to do?

Following are a few examples of forces, trends and events that might affect your industry and your business.

Example: Plausible Scanning Events

STEEP	World	National	Local
Social	Religious, terrorist wars Mass immigration	Religious, terrorist, political events Medical care cost or availability Shootings	Shortage of workers and personnel Doctor shortage
Technology	Biotech and medical breakthroughs Automated Intelligence (AI) Robotics	Change in production tech (robotics) Change in delivery or logistics tech (3D)	Local technology training Internet competition
Economic	Business cycle downturn Strengthening or weakening markets	Business cycle downturn Taxation change Strikes or potential strikes against your industry or transportation industry.	Taxation change Incentives
Ecologic	Global warming	Global warming Air, water pollution	Air, water pollution Flooding risk Wildfire risk

Political	Wars	Elections Tax changes Militancy Immigration	Local elections Incentives to build or hire in some communities.

Figure 6.3- Examples of scanning events that might impact your business.

Which of these groups of forces are likely to have a strong impact on your business at one or more of these geographic levels, and how? Futurists refer to this process as "360 degree scanning" to emphasize the importance of looking all around you to see what is happening and what appears to be changing. Recommended sources include online-media, newspapers, newsletters, journals, speeches, magazines, television, and any source that might reliably and intelligently warn of change.

Everything is connected!

One of the difficulties with anticipating the future is that nearly everything is related to everything else, so when one element of society or of your business changes, other parts may change as well. As you explore change in the world around you, consider how trends in one category might impact other categories.

For example: if prices of basic household commodities such as flour, soap, beans, and spices rise in a developing country, the people with the least money are likely to be affected the most.

So the economy has changed, becoming more expensive.

How will that affect subsistence farmers and others with little cash? Suppose, to earn more income, the farmers start cutting down trees to sell the logs for lumber and the limbs for firewood. That will give the farmers cash and more land to farm. However, logging inflicts damage to the ecosystem, removing habitat for animals, removing oxygen generators (trees), and disturbing the soil. In addition, the logs have to be transported by roads or waterways, resulting in additional impacts.

 The farmers are now seeing the economic benefits of selling logs and firewood, so they invest in new (for them) technology, chain saws, and eventually tractors.

The impacts of the logging now attract the attention of ecologists in other parts of the world who raise the alarm about the bad things that can happen as a result of this trend. Enter the politicians. They now have a constituency (farmers, truck drivers, chainsaw importers and others) who can vote!

Very quickly, all five of the STEEP categories are involved in this scenario, creating trends in each.

The same thing is true in your business domains. A change in one domain will probably affect other domains.

The Finances domain directly affects every other domain in your business. As long as you have good financial conditions in your business, all of the other domains are impacted in a positive way.

One more force—Values

Everyone has values. Values represent what each of us believe— what's right, what's wrong, what we want to achieve, and what we feel is important. Each person should be aware of their personal values as well as the values of any business partners.

If one partner or influential person in the business believes it is okay to lie, or to steal, or to be cruel, how will those values affect the business? If the business has several partners or key persons, how will those multiple sets of values impact the business?

Among potential owners of a new business, personal values and the values of the new business are often not considered. Personal values are frequently treated as personal and private. The problem with that approach is that when the business reaches a crisis that is related to values, ethics, or morality, owners have no common moral background to call upon.

One solution is for the partners/owners/management to agree on a set of values and state them publicly, either as values or as ethics. Searching for "business values" on Google may confuse you, but the various lists will give you some clues.

It is also worthwhile to be aware of the values and ethics of suppliers, stakeholders and clients, as their values could affect your business in the future.

On the following page are a few examples to consider as you think about values and ethics in your business:

Accountability	Idealism
Balance	Improvement
Collaboration	Innovation
Communication	Integrity
Competitive Spirit	Job Satisfaction
Compliance	Keep commitments
Continuous Improvement	Leadership
Courage	Learning
Customers	No fine print
Dedication	Openness,
Discipline	Partnership
Diversity	Passion
Do the right thing	Quality
Educate	Respect
Empathy	Responsibility
Employee welfare	Safety
Environment	Self-Discipline
Ethical	Self-Improvement
Exceeding expectations	Self-Respect
Excellence	Sustainably
Fairness	Teamwork
Generosity	Trustworthy
Good citizens	Unselfishness
Have fun	Values
Honesty	
Humility	

Whether your business has one owner or many, it is valuable to put your values on paper. They are a measure of your aspirations and your morality.

In the next chapter, you will explore events that may occur in your business simply because similar events have occurred to other small businesses. You will be learning about the future of your business from people and organizations that have already experienced it!

CHAPTER 7

Events That Will Impact or Change Your Business

Concept

Events that may occur in the future can be categorized in several different ways— positive/negative, high impact/low impact, turning-point, growth, legal, and intentional/unintended events are some categories. Some events will have serious impacts and others will be routine. Understanding events and their relationships to your business will be helpful as you navigate your way into the future.

Events

Many events occur during the life of each business. Many events can be anticipated, whether because they are common in most businesses, or because they are the result of expected individual actions or behaviors. Events also vary in degree of impact, so it makes sense to focus on the events that will have the greatest impacts on your business.

Things happen. Good things, bad things; expected and unexpected; accidental and intentional. In this chapter, you are going to explore some of the events that may occur in your business in the future. Bracketing is a simple technique that can help you anticipate some events that may be ahead for your business.

Bracketing can be very useful for events and changes that are related to the stages of development your business will encounter over time. You can bracket an event by identifying the earliest date and the latest date that event could occur, so the event should happen sometime between those dates. As you get nearer to the anticipated event, you may be able to narrow the time range and see clues as to when the event will actually happen.

For example, I live near the Gulf Coast of Texas, so we have to be concerned about hurricanes each year. The annual hurricane season starts in June and ends in November. Those are my big brackets, but experience tells me that the greatest concern will be in July through September, giving me the smaller brackets. Once the hurricane season starts, I pay attention to the weather reports of tropical storms forming in the Atlantic and moving toward the Gulf. If a storm enters the Gulf, I pay more attention to the forecasts of the storm's path. If the storm develops as a hurricane and keeps moving in our direction, I start making preparations to secure our home and business, and to leave the area.

The same approach works with many events, even those that seem far away. Exiting your business is an event that may be far off in the future, but you know that it will have to happen. If you start thinking about your exit now, you can take steps in each of your domains over the years ahead to assure that you will be prepared when the event or opportunity arrives.

Types of Events

Turning point events

Turning point events change the direction or even the nature of your business. Google, for example, came into existence as a search engine, then began selling advertising and search words. Today, Google has reorganized its business and changed its name to Alphabet. Among other projects, Google/Alphabet is developing a self-driving car, a potential turning point for the company.

Apple started business developing and manufacturing computer kits for hobbyists, then personal computers. In 2001, Apple introduced the iPod, then iTunes, and iPhones and now the Apple watch. All are turning point events because they change the direction or nature of the business.

A possible turning point in international diplomacy when, in 2018, the U.S government initiated actions to withdraw from some international agreements, to renegotiate other agreements, to reduce illegal immigration and to change international business relationships, including new or increased tariffs. These actions impacted many businesses, changing costs and competition.

Growth events

There are many types of events related to the growth of a business. A restaurant or retail store may remodel or expand. Small manufacturers may move from their roots in a garage into a rented space and eventually into a building of their own. When a small company has grown enough to be ready to go public, that is truly a growth event.

Legal events

Legal events are based on documents, laws or legislation. Signing a partnership agreement, incorporating a business, applying for a sales tax number, or filing a tax return are all legal events. Every business transaction has legal implications.

Intentional or choice events

Many turning-point events are the result of intent or choice, but people and businesses make smaller decisions and choices every day. Many of those choices have impacts on the future. Some examples are: decisions about extending credit to customers, use of debt, and investments in equipment, personnel or inventory. Those may each be small decisions at the time they are made, but they may lead to sizable impacts, positive or negative. Sometimes you will make deliberate decisions to change something in your business or set goals for something that you want to achieve in the future.

Unintended events

Sometimes, actions taken by the business or the owners may have consequences that are not intended or expected. Sometimes the consequences are the result of myopia—not thinking through to see the effects of an action, or rushing to take action.

Example: Three partners form a business, agreeing that no partner can take a draw during the first year or before the business makes a profit (an action to protect cash flow). Six months after the business is up and running, one partner with critical skills to the business decides he/she cannot continue without an income, and resigns.

Losing one or more customers, employees, partners, or advisors is usually not intentional, but it happens. In addition, injuries may occur to customers or employees. These are never intentional, but often have consequences.

Wild card events

A wild card event is an event that has a low probability of occurring, but when it happens there is a very high impact. Natural disasters such as hurricanes, floods, fires, and earthquakes are all considered to be low probability events, but when they occur, when they hit your place of business, they carry a very high impact.

In your business, extremely high or sudden demand for your products or services could be a wild card event, especially if it catches you unprepared.

Impacts of Events on Your Business

Some events will have powerful impacts on you and your business. For example, acquiring or losing a large customer, being sued, or moving your business to a new location are each high-impact events. Yet other events will have little or no impact at all.

How do you recognize or define impacts? Are there different types? On the next page is a list examples of plausible events that may happen in your business. Look at the first item, "Accept credit cards". Sounds simple, even necessary in many businesses, but there will be impacts, starting with extra costs and risks of fraud. On the other hand, there will probably be increased sales and transactions made simpler for your clients or customers.

In short, think about the future impacts of potential events, large and small.

Accept credit cards
Audit
Be sued
Big Storm
Borrow money
Build business location
Business destroyed
Business fails
Buy business location
Buy insurance
Company car stolen
Company car wrecked
Computer crash
Computers hacked
Create a business plan
Create a marketing plan
Create a strategic plan
Create a web site
Create a web store
Create quality control
Customer lists stolen
Customer(s) injured by product
Design marketing materials
Develop new product
Develop new service

Discover competitor
Earthquake
Employee dies at work
Employee fails drug test
Employee injured on job.
Employee killed on job
Employee retires
Equipment loss
Establish retirement plan
Establish standards
File bankruptcy
Find a business location
Fire
Fire an employee
First sale
Flood
Fraud by employee
Hacked
Hire a Consultant
Hire a contractor
Hire a marketing manager
Hire a sales manager
Hire an Accountant
Hire an Attorney
Hire first employee
Hire IT pro
Hurricane

Install computer system
Key person sick
Lease business location
Lose customer
Lose money
New large customer
Participate in tradeshow
Partner retires
Pay taxes
Power loss
Prepare loan application
Production problem
Receivable loss
Register business
Rent business location

Reputation at risk
Sales growth
Sales problem
Send press release
Start advertising
Start blog
Start drug testing
Sue someone
Tax audit
Terrorist attack
Theft by employee
Theft by intruder
Train new employee
Vandalism
Web site hacked

Each of these events can have different meanings and different impacts for individuals and businesses of any size. The reason for this long list of events is to give you the opportunity to consider common events and whether an event might occur in your business. Now, long before the event occurs, is the time to ask yourself, "If or when this event occurs, how will I deal with it?" Anticipation of future events is a way to reduce the number of surprises, particularly the negative ones.

A personal Experience

A friend and I experienced a different kind of event when we developed a line of ski waxes— sticks of wax that downhill skiers, from beginners to racers, rubbed on the bottoms of their skis to make them faster and smoother in different snow conditions. Our waxes contained Teflon, a new product at that time. The waxes were easy to apply, and worked much better than existing products. We hired a design firm and developed special packaging in zip-lock bags, which were also new at that time.

Skiers and marketers loved the product and predicted great success. We introduced our waxes (mid 1960s) at the same winter sports marketing event where several prominent ski manufacturers introduced their new skis— all with *no-wax* finishes on the running surface, a revolutionary development! We had a great product with excellent appeal, but most skiers would no longer need to apply wax to their skis!

One of the objectives of exploring the future is to avoid being blindsided. That is why it is important to consider, explore, and look for events that could hurt you or your business.

The following worksheet, Figure 7.1 suggests a number of events that could occur during different stages of the development of a small business. These examples are intended to help you think about possible events in the future as your business changes.

Common and High Impact Events

Business Stage	Common events	High impact events
Concept	Idea Proof of concept Available target	Opportunity offered.
Planning	Prove long term viability. Business plan Structure (Corporation, Partnership, or Proprietorship).	Finance approval/disapproval.
Startup	First production. Work out bugs. First sales.	Very low sales. Extremely high sales.
Struggling	Not enough buyers. Cash flow problem. Inadequate funding. Taxes.	Rejections/returns. Loss of funding/partner. Loss of supplier. Loss of receivables.
Growth	Increasing demand. Supply problems. Logistics problems.	Quality control. Materials shortages.
Maturity	Slower growth.	Very strong competition.
Decline	Reduced sales. Reduced profit. Low demand.	Negative profit. Declining value of assets.
Exit	Sale. Transfer. Close.	Tax problem. Foreclosure.

Figure 7.1- Examples of events that may occur at different stages of development in a small business.

Wild cards and high impact events

Wild card events are low-probability events that are unlikely to happen in your business, but they could.

Internal Forces	High Impact examples
Finances	Very large receivables loss, large employee theft, lawsuit loss. Fire, flood, or natural disaster. Large, profitable opportunity, sale, or new product. IRS audit.
Location	Fire, explosion, earthquake, flood, hurricane, government taking, major utilities failure. Change in zoning, traffic patterns or neighboring businesses.
Operations	Major quality control failure. Innovative method or process. Automation or robotics.
Management	Blunder, theft, partner revolts or departs. Management becomes a very effective team. Hacked! Sued!
Marketing	Marketing/sales failure, product made obsolete, loss of THE major customer. Major marketing/sales success.
People	Major injuries or illness, strike, lack of work. Entire organization works together effectively.

Figure 7.2- What are the uncertainties in your business? Think about the most important uncertainties that you might have to deal with.

Probable Events

What is the probability of *any* event happening, and which events are important?

The list of events above includes a lot of high-impact events, and some of those events may happen to your business over the next ten years. Take a few minutes to go back over the list in Figure 7.2. For each event in the list, assign a rating for the next ten years using a scale of one (not at all likely) to five (will almost certainly happen). This will get you started thinking about probabilities and possibilities, and will provide you with lists of events that you will need in later chapters.

Not all high-probability events will be important as you plan for the future. Impact is usually more important. For example, the anniversary of the start of your business is a high-probability event, but it is not very useful in planning for your future (unless you plan to celebrate the event as a marketing celebration).

You may have to file tax reports monthly, quarterly, and annually, but these high-probability events generally do not have much impact on your business (unless you fail to file!).

In summary, many different types of events will impact your business over the years ahead. Thinking about events and trying to anticipate when or if any of those events will occur is valuable, because it keeps you thinking about the future.

In the next chapter, you will learn to use a tool that is a favorite among futurists: the two-axis matrix.

CHAPTER 8

The Two-axis Matrix

Concept

Very simple, yet very effective, the two-axis matrix is helpful in comparing the impacts of forces and determining the importance of events now and in the future.

A favorite tool of futurists

This is a tool you can use anywhere—on a pad of paper, a napkin, or your computer. You can plot a single event or many events in one diagram, which is based on two simple scales. In our example, the scales will be Impact and Probability. Assuming this is your first experience with a two-axis matrix, here is how it works:

Rate an event on both scales from 1 to 5. In this case, the lowest Probability or Impact would be 1 and the highest Probability or Impact would be 5. This example assumes a specific event has a probability of occurring, ranked at 5, and an impact of 4.

The "X" in the upper right quadrant of the diagram shows the intersection of the two forces.

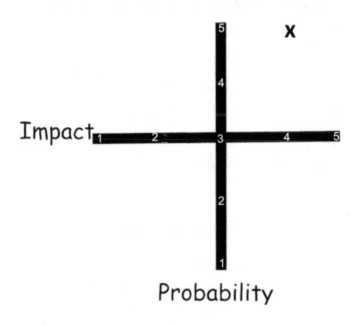

Figure 8.1 – Rating multiple events on the two-axis matrix.

In order to put several events into one diagram using the same two axes (forces), just make a numbered list of events that you think might occur in the next ten years, then position each number into the two-axis matrix based on that number's impact and probability. For example

1. Create a website
2. Hire an accountant
3. Fire an employee
4. New large customer/client
5. Lose important customer/client
6. Theft by an employee

7. Hire a contractor
8. Be sued
9. Pay taxes
10. Computer crash

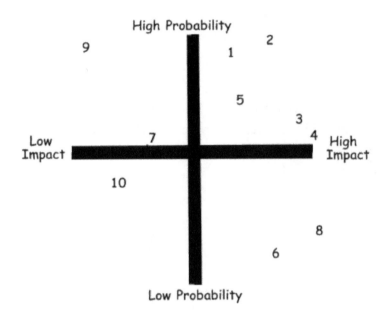

Figure 8.2 – The ten plausible events listed above are shown in the four quadrants of a two-axis matrix. The position in the matrix of each number indicates the probability the event will occur and the expected impact of that event on a business. Number 4 suggests a medium probability of "new, large customer or client" but a very high impact if that event occurs.

Notice the number of events (1, 2, 3, 4, 5) in the upper-right quadrant, which combines high probability with high impact. These are events that will have a strong impact, and will probably occur in a hypothetical business. Consequently, you should not only be prepared for these events to happen but should develop strategies and a plan for dealing with each of them.

VERNE WHEELWRIGHT

The events in the lower-right quadrant (6, 8) also have a high impact but are not likely to happen. Yet, you should be aware of these possibilities, have a contingency plan, and be prepared to deal with them if they do occur. In the upper-left quadrant are events (7, 9) that will probably happen, but will not have much impact on your business. In the lower-left quadrant are the events (10) that probably will not happen and would not have much impact on your business if they did.

Now that you see how to put plausible future events into a matrix, you may be wondering why you are going through this exercise. The next diagram will help explain. Each sector or quadrant in the matrix indicates the type of planning for the future for that quadrant.

Figure 8.3 - This matrix suggests planning needs for events in each quadrant. You will see this diagram again in the strategic-planning section.

This is a diagram to remember. It identifies how you should deal with future events in each of the four quadrants.

Routine Planning This quadrant is for events you put on your calendar or planner such as birthdays, anniversaries, appointments, and meetings.

Strategic Planning In this quadrant, you will have high-impact, high-probability events. You will need to prepare for these events, developing strategies and plans so that you have a clear idea of how you are going to deal with each.

Contingency Planning This is the area for wild cards and high-impact, low-probability events. For each event, you should consider a contingency plan to have in place in case the event occurs.

Planning Not Necessary The heading says it all. There is no need to make plans for events that are unlikely to occur and that have little or no impact if they do occur.

Forces as Axes in a Two-axis Matrix

How do you pick the forces that become the axes on your matrix?

Ask yourself, "Which forces are driving change in your business?" For a young business, sales are not only important but critical, both to the survival of the business and to growth, so that's a good place to start.

For example, the diagram below looks at Awareness and Acceptance of your products or services. First, you are being asked if your potential customers are aware of your products—do they know your products exist?

On the other axis, do potential customers like or want your products?

Once you identify where your products fit on the matrix, you will have to decide what it will take to create change.

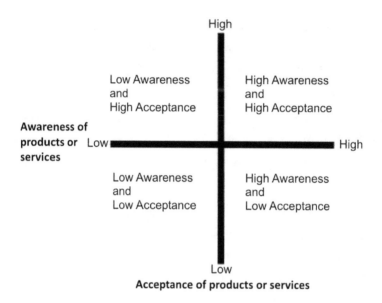

Figure 8.4- In this case, the matrix is used to consider or analyze a problem that directly relates to sales. Obviously, businesses want to be in the upper right quadrant where both Awareness and Acceptance are high.

Are potential customers aware of your products and how to obtain them (and how do you know)? Do potential customers who know about your products accept them for quality and price (again, how do you know)? If you have multiple products or services, make a numbered list, then place the number for each product on the diagram.

Assuming that you want all your products to appear in the upper right corner, what do you need to do to get them there?

1.   Determine where, on this matrix, one or more of your products or services is offered by your business now.
2.   Decide where you want this product or service to be on the matrix in the future.
3.   Create strategies to achieve #2.
4.   Repeat for other products.

Diagrams like this are very useful, but after you have identified highs and lows in the four quadrants for several forces, you will realize there should be something with more depth. The next step includes analysis of two forces on the matrix and determining what the positions in the quadrants actually represent.

How do you chose the two forces to put into the matrix? To start, look at the six small business domains (Internal Forces) in the chart below. In the diagram, the second column is "Examples" of forces at work in each of the domains. Any or many of these examples may be of interest or concern in your business. Pick any two that are of interest to you at this moment from the second column.

Internal Forces

Internal Forces	Examples
Finances	Capital, cash flow, income, assets, expense, debt, liabilities, financial risks, insurance, taxes, accounting.
Location	Building, facilities, zone, neighborhood, languages, city, state or province, country.
Operations	Production of goods or services, processes, materials, quality control, logistics, inventories.
Management	Legal structure, organizational structure, core business, divisions, legal and regulatory requirements.
Marketing	Sales, customer relations, publicity, promotions, advertising.
People	Owners, staff, employees, advisors, suppliers, contractors.

Figure 8.5- Examples of internal forces at work in your business.

How can you use this information to think about the future? Let's start by picking one of the examples from the table above, "Sales", since every business needs sales. That will be the horizontal line of your matrix.

Every business also has cash flow so we can label the vertical line Cash Flow, adding Low at the bottom and High at the top. In each quadrant, ask yourself what the future impact will be of sales to cash flow. For example, in the upper left quadrant, the relationship between low sales and high cash flow might be the result of very high margins.

What does that mean to you as far as planning for the future? If you expect very low sales volume (left quadrants), you will probably want to price your products or services high in order to achieve high margins (upper left quadrant), which you will probably need in order to keep your business successful.

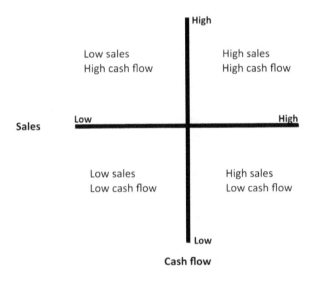

Figure 8.6- A matrix exploring Cash Flow and Sales. Where would your business fit on this matrix?

In the lower right quadrant of the matrix, if you find that your business is suffering from low cash flow, even though you have high sales, you may have to review your sales terms or your enforcement of collections in order to keep your cash flow at a supportable level.

The preferred quadrant for most businesses is the upper right quadrant with "High cash flow and high sales." Where is your business represented on this matrix today? What strategies will you need to improve those positions?

STEEP forces

Chapter 6 introduced the STEEP forces, the forces that are external to your business, and that change the world around you. Any consideration of the future of your business must include those forces.

External (STEEP) Forces	Plausible Examples
Social	Immigration, Extreme longevity, Genomics, CRISPR, Bio medicine, Robotics and automation.
Technology	Self-driving vehicles, 3D printing and distribution, robotics and automation. Virtual reality.
Economics	Global currency, Blockchain, Developing economies becoming developed. Business cycle – Recession, Business cycle- Recovery.
Ecology	Global warming, water scarcity, wildfires, extreme weather.
Politics	Terrorism, robotics and automation, international trade.

Figure 8.7- The STEEP categories and examples of plausible and probable change.

Notice that in the STEEP forces, "robotics and automation" are listed as examples in three different categories. Obviously, robotics and automation are part of technology, but these technologies will certainly impact the Social sector if workers lose their jobs or if elderly people can receive care in their own homes through advancing technologies. In turn, the Political sector may be impacted, as workers who have lost their jobs will demand solutions or compensation.

How do these forces in the world impact each other, and how may they impact your business?

Let's start with the business cycle. Figure 8.7 lists the Business Cycle, both as a recession and a recovery, and a cycle that usually lasts about ten years. That makes an economic downturn a high probability event over the next ten years, which suggests that you need to be prepared for the economy to fall at nearly any time. If you know that a recession is in your future, what can you do with that knowledge? Consider what usually happens when the economy overheats, then collapses.

- Sales fall off or at least slow down. Prices may drop.
- Collections of receivables slow down, become more difficult to collect, and in some cases become uncollectible.
- Inventories lose value. If goods are in transit, buyers may refuse to accept goods or insist on renegotiating the price.

Now, you know something about the future. You know there will be a business downturn—you just don't know when! But, you can protect yourself and your business in some ways, largely by following good business practices and staying aware of what the future could be for your business. Always.

The next chapters will consider SWOT—Strengths, Weaknesses, Opportunities, and Threats, all of which will impact the future of your business.

CHAPTER 9

Your Business:

Strengths, Weaknesses, Opportunities, and Threats

Concept

SWOT is an analytical tool that helps individuals and organizations analyze characteristics that will strongly influence change in the future. Analysis of each of the four SWOT areas starts preparing you to not only anticipate the future but to realistically prepare for and deal with future events.

L ater in this chapter is another tool, the Futures Wheel (or mind map), which is very useful for analyzing concepts, systems, and ideas or for brainstorming with others.

SWOT

SWOT stands for strengths, weaknesses, opportunities, and threats. This is a tool that has been successfully used in strategic planning for decades. Now you have an opportunity to see how effective this tool is when you to your small business.

This is a good system, and you should give some serious thought to each of the four categories.

Starting with a blank page does not do much to stimulate thinking, so we are going to take a more direct approach that will give you more clues and more to think about. First, think of strengths and weaknesses as *internal* concerns, strictly about your business. Next, think of opportunities and threats as *external* concerns from the world around you.

Strengths and Weaknesses

Start with the strengths of your business, then explore weaknesses, and look at them in each of your six domains. Figure 9.1 shows some examples of both strengths and weaknesses that a person might recognize in his or her own business. In each of these tables you will find a few brief examples to help get you started.

Strengths and Weaknesses

Domain	Strengths	Weaknesses
Finance	Adequate funds for two years. Customers agree to fast terms in return for priority delivery.	One large customer is asking for longer terms.
Location	Low rent. Good location.	Not attractive!
Marketing	Potential customers are very web savvy, easy to reach. Strong marketing team knows market.	Vulnerable to negative feedback if we make a mistake. Weakness in international experience.
Operations	Owners are very skilled in this business.	Equipment is outdated. Weak quality control.
Management	Good team, mostly very experienced. Long term focus. Very strong patent protection.	Owners not strong in financial management.
People	Core group of REALLY good people.	Not trained in cyber security.

Figure 9.1-A worksheet for Strengths and Weaknesses.

When you divide the question about your strengths into the six domains, the answers become very specific and are less vague or complex. Keep in mind that it is okay to break any domain down into smaller parts.

You may have strengths in any (or many) of these areas. For example, substantial capital and strong cash inflow are valuable strengths in the Finance domain. A good location and low rent are strengths in the Location domain. Customers and prospects who are accessible on the Internet may be a strength for the Marketing domain, as are skills and an experienced individual to manage sales and marketing. If you or any partners are very experienced, skilled, or knowledgeable in operations, that is a definite strength. A long term perspective is a valuable attribute to the Management domain, and people who are trustworthy, involved, and enthusiastic about the success of your business are valuable strengths and assets to all the domains. The point is that you should look carefully at *all* of your strengths and recognize them for what they are.

Now comes the hard part: recognizing your weaknesses. Part of the value of this exercise is that once you recognize a weakness, you can do something about it. One of the risks in a small business is ignoring problems or weaknesses, hoping they will fix themselves. They never do!

Small businesses usually start out with one obvious weakness—the owners/managers don't know everything that would be useful and helpful to the business. That's not bad, simply realistic.

A common weakness in small business is in the Finance domain. Inadequate capital and slow or negative cash flow head the list. Poor records-keeping (accounting) is close behind. It's exciting to make and sell products or services, but many small businesses don't make the time to keep good records or keep close track of both income and expenses until it is time to file a required report or tax return. That weakness in the Finance area means that the Management domain (owners and managers), lack up-to-date information on the finances of the business to monitor financial positions or make good decisions about the business.

In the Marketing domain, a common weakness might occur when too much attention is given to one or two good customers. A customer or client who buys a lot of your product or service is wonderful—until that customer stops buying.

Small businesses very often rely entirely on the experience or expertise of the owner(s), whereas large organizations are able to hire experienced professionals in every area of the business.

Acknowledging and recognizing your weaknesses will help you deal with or even overcome many of them.

This process for analyzing your strengths and weaknesses continues through all six domains, giving you a well-rounded picture of all aspects of your business. This analysis also has the benefit of drawing your attention to what you need to change and to identifying the strengths you can put to use.

Next, you will explore the external factors in your business: opportunities and threats. Again, you will break these categories down into the major driving forces in the world around you, the STEEP categories we explored in Chapter Eight.

Opportunities

Notice that the columns in figures 9.2 and 9.3 encourage you to think about each of the categories on a global, national, and local basis. Global and national forces will often appear to be vague or distant and out of your control, while local forces are likely to have the most direct impacts on your business.

Opportunities at Three Levels

External Opportunities	Global	National	Local
Social	Need exists for our products worldwide.		Major University and two technical schools in area.
Technology		Access to good transportation.	Good, educated labor pool available.
Economy		Strong national economy. Have confirmed, long term buyers.	Traditionally low labor and living costs.
Ecology		Does our packaging affect the ecology?	
Politics			Local government will provide incentives to locate here.

Figure 9.2- A worksheet for Opportunities.

Starting with opportunities, what are the opportunities that you see in each STEEP category and in each of the three geographic areas over the next ten years? At first you might wonder about the opportunities in global change. New or advancing technologies may work for you or against you. Robotics, artificial intelligence, self-driving vehicles, and medical science are all promising substantial change in the future, but how will they impact you and your business? Are you threatened? Do you see emerging opportunities?

A growing global economy may improve your business opportunities. Reduced political tensions and conflicts also increase opportunities for businesses of all sizes.

When you bring the forces of change down to the local level, it is easy to see the direct impacts on your business. Considerable information about the future may be found in local planning department records and plans for future development. If the city where your business is located is planning to install larger water mains near your building that could lower your fire insurance rates. If the police department is planning a substation near your business, that could reduce crime and raise valuations. If your community improves streets, lighting, or drainage in the area around your business, that could increase traffic and raise the value of your business location (or raise your rent!).

Improving the status of your business in the future is what this exercise is all about. Thinking seriously about your future is the best way to improve the long term health of your business.

Threats

Now for the threats. What do you see in the world, your country, or your community that threatens the future of your business over the next ten years or longer?

Threats at Three Levels

External Threats	Global	National	Local
Social	Religious wars. Nationalism.	Political battles. Growing unemployment.	Increasing homeless population.
Technology	Nuclear terror threat. Lawless Internet. AI/Robotics replacing lower level workers.	Shortage of high skilled workers. AI/Robotics a threat to workers.	Very high wages.
Economy	Business curve turns down. China downturn. Political disruptions.	Business curve turns downward. Tax increase. Crumbling infrastructure.	Tax increases. Lack of trained workers.
Ecology	Global warming. Rising oceans. Shrinking fisheries.	More and larger wildfires.	Local air and water pollution.
Politics	Breakdown of alliances. Potential trade wars.	Increased divisions between parties.	Crumbling infrastructure.

Figure 9.3- Threats at three levels— Local, National and International.

It is sometimes hard to see how threats on the other side of the world might affect you, but if your country is involved in any way, even in simply defending against those threats, your personal and business taxes are probably affected. Conflicts around the world may restrict your opportunities, may impact your travel choices, or may increase general tensions.

It may be hard to see how you should be concerned about global warming, but if you see your community running low on water, suffering from wildfires, or dealing with very severe weather, the impacts become more obvious. It seems clear that a trade war, in which countries raise tariffs on imports could impact your business, whether raising the cost of raw materials or increasing the cost of your products to overseas buyers.

That, briefly, is SWOT. It is a tool that will help you think about change as you think about the future. Just listing your strengths, weaknesses, opportunities, and threats is sufficient to get you thinking, but there is more. Look at your strengths to see how they match up with your opportunities. How can you use those strengths to enjoy the benefits of the opportunities that you have listed? What can you do to change what you perceive as your weaknesses? If you lack experience or education in any area, can you get training, go back to school, or take courses online to change that weakness to a strength? Those decisions will change your future.

In the next section of this chapter, you will learn about the Futures Wheel, a very useful tool for exploring the present and the future.

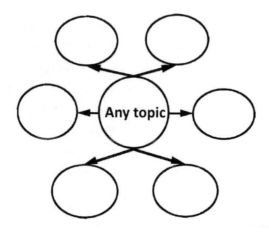

The Futures Wheel

Figure 9.4- The Futures Wheel, a valuable tool for exploring the present and the future.

The Futures Wheel is a tool that is used by most futurists. It is also called a mind map, and can be very simple, like the example above.

At the same time, Futures Wheels can become complex as more levels are added, They are very effective for brainstorming, whether you are working alone or in a group. You can draw one anywhere— on paper, on a whiteboard or in your computer.

Building a Futures Wheel

Figure 9.5- A basic business Futures Wheel showing spaces for the first level of forces.

The idea is to start with a question, situation, or problem, then branch out from that idea to directly link to related ideas, effects, impacts or whatever you are considering. From that level, branch out again.

The Futures Wheel is versatile. You will find it helpful in sorting out ideas or simply thinking about the future or other concepts. If you have occasion to speak to a group of people, the Futures Wheel is a great tool for brainstorming and collecting ideas or information. All you need is a blank space and something you can write with.

To start a Futures Wheel, state your question, problem, or starting point of interest in the center circle, then identify the characteristics, questions, impacts or thoughts that you associate with the central question in the surrounding circles as seen in Figure 9.5.

A Second level of impacts

Figure 9.6- From the basic Futures Wheel, extend outward to create another ring, or second level of impacts.

From each of the domains in the first ring around your business, extend to secondary ideas or impacts. From there, branch out to the third ring and so on. When you are drawing on paper or a whiteboard, Futures Wheels start getting messy at this level, but they still work!

A Third level of impacts

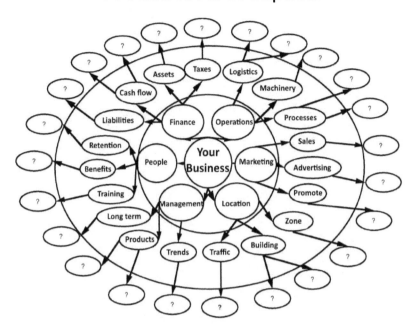

Figure 9.7- The Futures Wheel expanded to another level of impacts.

Futures Wheels are effective for thinking about the future or just sorting through questions or problems, either on your own or with a group. They are *very* effective in brainstorming sessions, as they allow you to record random thoughts that can be tied into the conversation.

You can start a Futures Wheel about your business with the six business domains, or you can go directly to a single domain or to a specific problem. Figure 9.8 starts from the Operations domain.

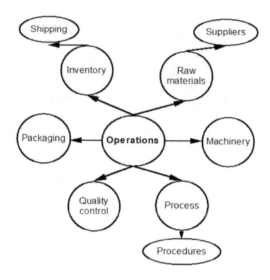

Figure 9.8- You can build a Futures Wheel from any of the domains of your business.

The next example starts in the Shipping and Receiving node of the Operations domain.

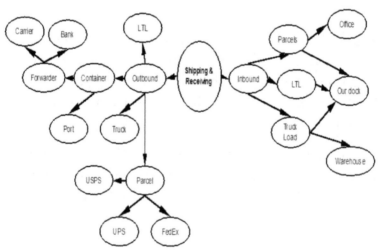

Figure 9.9- In this example, the Futures Wheel is expanded from one node of the Operations domain to explore some of the options available to the Shipping and Receiving department.

The Futures Wheel can be used to diagram the past, the present, or the future. The diagram above shows present options, but could just as well be used to include future options, or consider the future options by themselves.

Figure 9.10 - This Futures Wheel adds technology that is still in the future, but could change the way you or your competitors do business.

These examples may not resemble your business, however the concepts are useful in almost any situation you wish to explore. The point here is simply that the Futures Wheel is flexible, and you can use it to explore or think through nearly any situation. Online, you can search for Futures Wheels, Mind Maps, and Implication Wheels for software and more ideas.

You will find the Futures Wheel helpful in sorting out ideas or simply thinking about the future or other concepts. If you have occasion to speak to a group of employees, visitors or customers, the Futures Wheel is a great tool for brainstorming and collecting ideas or information or for explaining whatever is happening.

In this chapter you have learned (or reviewed) how to use two important tools that will help you to understand more about your business and your future:

SWOT analysis- a close look at your strengths, weaknesses, opportunities and threats.

The Futures Wheel—how to diagram almost anything about your business.

What you have learned will be very useful in the next sections, the chapters on developing scenarios and personal strategic planning.

Creating Scenarios for a Small Business

You have now explored your business and some of the potential trends and forces that will guide or impact your business in the future. In Section Two, you will consider potential futures using scenarios, a methodology developed and used by futurists over several decades.

Exploring plausible futures is the core method used by professional futurists to consider and prepare for the future. This exploration brings the important elements of the future together and in perspective.

CHAPTER 10

Scenarios: How Futurists Explore Alternate Futures

Concept

The scenario method is based on the theory of alternate futures. Stated simply:

"The future is not totally predetermined."

I f the future is not fully predetermined, then more than one future must be available.

Based on this concept, this chapter will help you to explore and construct four or five different types of futures. The basic events in each of these futures may be the same, but the scenarios will be changed by differences in the driving forces in your business or in the world around you.

Herman Kahn is credited with originating the scenario method during the 1950s, but the successful use of scenarios by Royal Dutch Shell on an international scale brought the scenario method to the attention of the business community and to governments worldwide. Peter Schwartz's 1991 book, *The Art of the Long View*, detailed one system for developing scenarios based on the Shell approach. This book is still on many futurists' bookshelves.

Before we go into more detail about scenarios, this is a good place to make an important point. The Chinese philosopher Lao Tzu wrote in the sixth century BC:

Those who have knowledge don't predict.

Those who predict don't have knowledge.

I include this quotation to emphasize that scenarios will teach you quite a bit about what *may* happen in the future, but they do not tell you what *will* happen. Scenarios are not predictions. Most futurists will agree that they cannot predict the future, but they are trained to make some pretty good guesses. That is what scenarios are meant to be, educated guesses about the future. What you have learned about your business and the future in Section One of this book provides the foundation upon which the scenarios for your business will be built.

Why would you use scenarios?

We use scenarios to *rehearse* the future. A scenario might be compared to a simulator. A simulator which trains people to deal with risky situations or to use high value equipment without risk to either the student or the equipment.

For example, in 1934, Ed Link demonstrated his Link Trainer to the Army Air Force, offering a way to teach pilots how to fly through bad weather using only the instruments in their airplane, probably the best early example of a simulator. The Link Trainers were important in teaching new pilots to fly during World War II without risk to pilots or aircraft. Today, sophisticated simulators let experienced pilots deal with low probability, high impact events in addition to helping new pilots learn the basics of maneuvers and instrument training. Beyond aviation, simulators now train people to operate ships, trains, trucks, cars, construction equipment, surgical devices and other high value equipment in high risk situations.

Similarly, scenarios let *anyone* explore and rehearse the future at low risk. You have the opportunity in developing scenarios to consider many possible situations and even more plausible solutions, using simple tools and a little imagination.

This entire section, Section Two, is about exploring the future. The many possible or plausible futures of your business.

Let's start with what a scenario is. First, scenario development is a method futurists use to explore plausible and wild card futures. Each scenario is a story about the future, say ten years (or longer) from now. Scenarios focus on actual knowledge, the knowledge that is available now, in the present. You will create alternative scenarios to deal with changes that may occur between now and the time of the scenario, for example, the next ten years.

 In this section on scenarios, you will be working with five different types of scenarios.

- A "continuation of the present into the future" scenario (described in Chapter 11).
This scenario assumes no major changes in the domains in your business during the next ten years.
- A "best plausible" scenario.
In this scenario, everything goes right for your business in each of the domains in your business. This scenario uses the *optimistic* projections for each of the domains.
- A "worst plausible" scenario.

In this scenario, everything goes wrong in your business. Here you will use the lower (negative) lines from the extrapolated for each of the six domains.

- A "wild card" scenario.

This scenario can be positive or negative and draws from events outside the cone of uncertainty for one of the six domains.

- An "aspirational" scenario.

This scenario is generally a positive event or outcome to which you or your business aspire. Often, the odds of success are against you, but hard work and perseverance may prevail. Building a "unicorn" (billion dollar valuation) business could be an example.

As mentioned earlier, there are at least a dozen recognized ways to create scenarios— some simple, some complex. We are going to use a simple approach that is quite effective, yet easy to understand and use. These scenarios will become plausible stories about the future—stories that *could* happen. Your business will be the main character in each scenario.

Each of your scenarios will be driven by forces of change. If you asked, you would probably find that most futurists use the two-axis matrix as an important tool in testing different forces against each other, identifying the logics for the final scenarios. Professional futurists usually consider a lot of potential scenarios, then write out the best in story form for each of the scenario types discussed above.

You will follow a similar but simpler route. The professional futurist is often working with an organization of thousands of people, while you will be making scenarios for your small business.

That gives you the advantage of simplicity and the power of decision making.

You will focus on five scenarios here, but you can consider as many as you want. After you have done the basic scenarios, try creating additional scenarios using the STEEP forces with each of the six domains. Be imaginative! Imagine the worst, then imagine the best. Imagine the surprises!

Bounding the future

Since scenarios are about understanding what may happen in the future, we try to put some boundaries on the future. We do this first with an optimistic scenario (the best plausible scenario) and then with a pessimistic scenario (the worst plausible scenario). The real future should lie somewhere between those two.

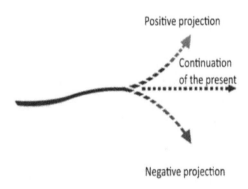

Figure 10.1- The cone of uncertainty is the space between the best and worst plausible projections. This is where positive and negative futures exist. The Wild card scenario and the Aspirational scenarios may be outside of these boundaries.

Be aware: The future will probably not match *any* of your scenarios! No matter how careful you are in crafting scenarios for your business, the future will very likely be different. The important thing to remember is that the value of the scenario is *not* precision. The goal is to make pathways into the future so that you can recognize where you are when you get there. If, as the future unfolds, you see that reality is more positive than the Extension of the Present scenario, but *not* as positive as the Optimistic scenario, you will recognize where reality is and how it compares with your scenarios.

What causes change in scenarios?

The challenge of scenario development is in looking from now into the future. The first question to ask is, "What *can* change?" Notice that question is asking "can," not "will." Nobody knows what *will* change, so keep asking, "What *can* change?" The next question is "Why?" In short, you want to know what can realistically change in the future, and what might cause that change to occur.

Primarily, change in your business will be created by forces— either internal forces (the six domains) or external forces (the STEEP categories). You have already looked closely at the six domains and (if you are using the workbook) have projected where those domains might go in the future and which domains are likely to dominate the next ten years.

The first scenario you develop will be one *without* any major change—just an extension of the present into the future. Certainly, there will be some change. You will get older, your business may move into another stage, and will pass through the normal events. In ten years, many things may be different, but they will also be familiar— no wrenching changes. This scenario without much change will give you a standard, a way to compare the other scenarios.

In the other scenarios, there will be change, and that change will be driven by the forces in one or two of the domains. For example, the Finances domain embraces everything related to money in your business. Finance is a dominant force during each stage of business growth and throughout the life of the business. So this is a good place to start asking yourself, "What could change?" What are the best things that could happen to finances in the business over the next ten years? What are the worst things that could plausibly happen?

Although we have focused on the internal domains of your business, because you have some control over those forces, you must pay attention to the STEEP forces, because what is happening in the world around you will impact your business. You may not be able to change these larger forces, but you can anticipate the impacts and prepare your business to deal with them.

Outside forces may impose change that will impact one or all of the domains. During 2008 and 2009, millions of people lost their jobs in a worldwide recession. Many small businesses lost their sources of funding as well as their customers. Businesses of all sizes collapsed, investments lost value, and many families lost their homes, their cars, and most of their possessions. Some small businesses received help from government programs, but many had no help at all. In the United States, large communities were formed by people living in tents because they had lost their homes. In China, workers in the cities returned to rural communities to stay with family and friends. Similar scenarios took place in much of the world.

That is an example of change—big, externally driven change. That is the important thing to look for in scenarios. What *could* change, and how would that change impact your business? What new or evolving technologies will impact your business? Robotics? Artificial intelligence? Cures for life threatening diseases like cancer or Alzheimer's? What if the human lifespan was extended to 150 years, or more?

Not all change is bad. As the world changes, new opportunities emerge. New customers, promotions, technologies or investments may appear. This is also change but in a positive direction, which illustrates why you make multiple scenarios. Try to anticipate the good things that can happen as well as the bad things that can impact the future of your business.

In the next chapter, you will learn how to set up information for each of your scenarios; then in the following chapter, you will see how changing forces impact your business, shaping the scenarios and the future of your business.

CHAPTER 11

Your Base Scenario

Concept

The base scenario assumes that during the time of the scenario, there are no major changes in the internal or external forces in your business, and that the driving forces continue moving in their present directions. This scenario provides the foundation for other scenarios in which the forces may be very positive, very negative, or changed by a wild card event (or your own aspirations).

An important decision you have to make about your scenarios is, "When will the scenario period end?" Are you exploring to the end of the Exit stage or for a set period, say the next ten years? What year will be the target year for the completion of your scenarios? The reason you need to decide on your target date now is that everything that will take place in your scenarios will happen between now and that target date. If you are undecided about the time period for your scenarios and your plan, use ten years. You can change this at any time.

With your target date for your scenarios in mind, this chapter will focus on the stages of growth and the events that may occur in those stages between now and your target date. This will become the foundation information for your business in each of your scenarios.

Stages

If you are using the *Small Business Foresight Workbook*, you will already have created the growth information for your business target year and identified any stakeholders who will be influential in your business over the next ten years (throughout, I will refer to ten years as the default time period.)

- Present stage

This is the stage your business is in today, which can be anywhere from the concept stage to approaching the Exit stage.

- Stages you expect to pass through during your scenario (the next ten years).

If you are in the Planning stage now, over the next ten years you might pass through the Startup and Struggling/Surviving stages, and into the Growth stage. Think about, and be realistic— how long do you expect your business to spend in each stage?

- Target stage
  The stage in which your business will be at the conclusion of your scenario.

Stakeholders and Change

Stakeholders are important! During the next ten years, the personal and business lives of your stakeholders will change, and some of those changes may have an impact on you and your business. You should be aware of the ages and life stages for each of the key people who are likely to influence your business from now until your target date. Assuming you have picked a target date ten years in the future, you already know that every person who will impact or influence your business will be ten years older than they are today. What you should be looking for here are the implications for each person, including you, of being ten years older. What changes or events will that ten-year period bring to their lives and yours? Do you have a college student working in your business now? In ten years, that student will have acquired a decade of experience and maturity. Do you have someone over age sixty in your organization or in a key position with a supplier, customer or competitor? What would be the impact on your business if one of those stakeholders retired or died?

Many people who are working in non-physical jobs are working well beyond the traditional retirement age. More important, older people bring with them a lifetime of experience, which may be valuable.

In your personal life, what life stage(s) will *you* be in and what will be different for you at your target date because of changes in your age and life stage? Obviously you will be a little older, a little more experienced, and probably noticing some physical changes if you are over fifty. What important events will happen in the lives of your spouse, your children, your parents, and other family members? If you have children, where will they be in *their* lives in ten years?

What ages and life stages will your parents and your spouse's parents be in at your target year? What will be the big events in their lives in ten years? Retirement? Health problems? Will you and your spouse have to help them in some way? What events in your parents' lives will impact your life? How will births, illnesses, deaths and other family events impact your business? And how will events in your business impact you and your family?

Your partners (if any), including spouses

What changes can you anticipate in your partners' lives? How is each partner likely to react to any of those changes? How might a

153

divorce, illness or death of a family member, or other major event affect that partner? How might events in a partner's life affect your business? How can you prepare to deal with the impacts?

Your employees

Are any of your employees or partners critical to your day to day operations? How would your business go on if one or more critical employees were absent for two weeks, a month or more?

Close advisors, consultants

Are critical advisors or consultants stable? Is there a backup? If your accountant, lawyer, loan officer or other individual is not available at a critical time, what will be the impact? Will any of your advisors retire during the next ten years?

Customers

Do you have any customers that are *very* important or even crucial to your business? If any one of your customers was unable to place orders or make payments for thirty days, sixty days, or even more, how would that impact your business?

Suppliers

Which suppliers of goods, materials or services are important or critical to your business? If any one of your suppliers was unable to meet your needs for thirty days or more, how would that impact your business? Do you have or need multiple or backup suppliers?

Look back over those last few paragraphs again and try to think about these stakeholders in your business and the effects that time or change may have on each of them, as well as on you and the future of your business.

Events

The information you develop from the Stages and Events worksheets will provide a foundation that will be the same in each of your scenarios. The differences between your scenarios will be determined by the driving forces in your business and in the world around you.

The Four Quadrants of the Impact/Probability Matrix

The matrix below, Impacts versus Probability, is worth remembering. For example, strategic planning for your business should focus on the upper right quadrant. This is where high impact, high probability events occur.

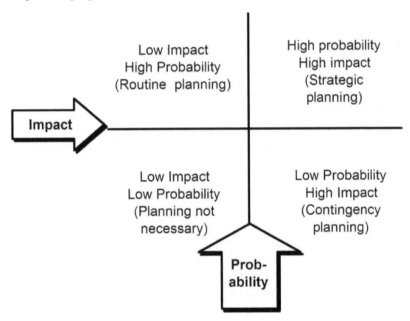

Figure 11.1 - Scenarios focus primarily on high-impact, high-probability events, while wild card scenarios are based on low-probability, high-impact events.

1. *Low-impact, low-probability events* (lower-left quadrant). These are the events that are unlikely to happen, but if they do, they will have very little impact on your business, so there is really no reason to plan or prepare for them. Example: It is common for small shipments, either inbound or outbound to be delayed or even lost. For most businesses, this is an annoyance, but not a serious problem. Many events are similar—they are not likely to happen but will have little or no impact if they do.

2. **Low-impact, high-probability events** (upper-left quadrant). Examples: appointments, meetings, holidays, vacations, etc. These are the events you put on your calendar, but they generally do not impact your business because they are routine. Completing, filing, and paying your taxes every year may be painful, but it is routine and low impact—unless you forget to file and get a visit from the tax collectors!

3. **High-probability, high-impact events** (upper-right quadrant). The events in this quadrant are the ones you will plan for and make strategies to deal with. These are the events that will appear in your scenarios and in your strategic plan. Examples: Gaining or losing a major customer/client, creating a new product, or advancing to a new stage of business are all examples of high-impact events that have a high probability of occurring.

4. **High-impact, low-probability events** (lower-right quadrant). Futurists call events in this quadrant wild cards. They are not likely to happen, but if they do, they may have a big impact on your business. These are the events that will appear in your contingency plan.

Some events may be hard to classify, and may be specific to your business or your location. Electric power outages are a good example. Some areas have frequent outages, some have very few. For some businesses, electric power twenty-four hours a day is critical, for other businesses electricity may be more of a convenience. The point here is that each business is different, and you will have to give considerable thought to defining "High Impact" for your business.

In parts of the world, terrorist acts or war are low-probability threats with devastating impacts. Natural events such as earthquakes, massive storms, wild fires or hurricanes may be events that occur only occasionally in the area where you live, but are threats that are always possible. I live near the Gulf Coast of Texas, where hurricanes are a threat every year. I have had a contingency plan for a long time, so when Hurricane Dolly struck in the summer of 2008, we were prepared with a plan and a backup.

Not all wild card events are negative, but disasters are the events that people tend to think of first. Natural disasters, low probability financial events (positive or negative), unexpected war or peace can all be seen as wild cards.

Starting a business that becomes a "unicorn" (a startup that becomes a billion dollar company, usually still privately held) could be a wild card or an aspiration, depending on your approach.

Such a scenario is a low probability, high impact situation that futurists consider an alternative or optional scenario. Aspirational scenarios are usually the result of setting a very high goal, then attempting to achieve it. Like the wild card, there is a low probability of success, but a big impact if successful. Charles

Lindberg's solo flight across the Atlantic in 1927 would be an example of a successful aspirational event.

"Extending the Present into the Future" — your foundation scenario

The main elements for your first scenario are the high-probability, high-impact events that may occur in your business over the next ten years. You can call this scenario an "extension of the present" scenario because it will *not* be driven by any of the forces of major change.

Following is an example of a scenario worksheet from the *Small Business Foresight Workbook*. There will be several more examples of worksheets in this and other chapters.

High Impact— High Probability Events

Internal Forces and Factors	Anticipated high impact and high probability events
Finance	Probability of economic downturn. Growing credit-worthiness (and profit). Building respect of suppliers and customers.
Location	Opportunities for better location(s). Lease deadline must be renewed or terminated.
Marketing	Increasing sales. Expanding markets.
Management	Gaining experience and sophistication in all areas.
Operations	Increasing production. Need for multiple suppliers. Quality control more important. Logistics becoming more important.
People	Increased staff. Standardize employee training. Train for greater responsibility. Increasing opportunities.

Figure 11.2- An example of a scenario worksheet showing high impact, high probability events for a small business. This worksheet, when completed, will suggest quite a bit about the next ten years. Note that the worksheets contain headlines only.

That is how you start your scenarios. Fill in a scenario worksheet, then write a story about the future of your business based on the worksheet information. Your first scenario (extending the present

159

into the future) becomes the foundation for all of your other scenarios. For each of the other scenarios, you will simply change this base scenario by adding one or two forces of change.

- One scenario will be driven by *positive change.*
- The next will be driven by *negative* change.
- (One will be driven by low-probability, *high-impact* change — a Wild card).
- One (optional) will be driven by your specific *aspirations* for your business.

You can probably see that the information in the table (Figure 11.2) and the details from your own knowledge about your business provide sufficient information for your scenario. From there, you will simply be writing a short story about possible futures for your business.

The next chapter will show how driving forces can change the futures for your business.

Driving Forces Will Change the Direction of Your Scenarios

Concept

The scenarios for your business are steered by the driving forces inside the business as well as the forces in the surrounding community and the world.

Beyond the base scenario

In this chapter, you are going to manipulate the future. Actually, what you manipulate will be your *views* of the future, but you will see how changes in the forces in your business can change the future of the business. Understanding how one set of forces can impact other forces to bring about change may give you a sense of understanding how the future works and how change comes about. That is good, and may demonstrate the value of these tools.

When you have completed the first scenario, "Continuation of the Present", you will continue with the same worksheet information that you developed for this scenario. This base information will be the same in all the scenarios for the future of your business. The differences between these scenarios will be in the forces that are driving your business—both the internal forces and the external forces.

Think about that for a second. Once you have identified which high-impact, high-probability events are likely to occur over the next ten years, those will be high-probability events no matter what else is happening. Whether your business is skyrocketing or failing, the high-probability events are still events that you must be prepared to deal with.

Some expected events may not happen. For example, new businesses usually have a period of struggling to make enough sales to support the business. However, if your business is filling an urgent need, sales and cash flow may develop quickly. Examples could include a dentist opening an office in an underserved community, or a technology business delivering a solution to an important problem such as malicious hacking or identity theft. At first, those examples suggest that those businesses might skip the Struggling/Surviving stage, but struggling involves more than cash flow, as a young business must be able to manage demand and delivery for its products and services.

Throughout this chapter, you will explore domains, the *internal* forces in your business, as well as the *external*, or STEEP forces discussed in Chapter Six.

The Positive Scenario

Your first scenario will be a positive scenario. The worksheet in figure 12.1 (below) has all of the same information as the worksheet for the Continuation of the Present Scenario. You will simply convert that information into a positive scenario by adding information about the forces in each domain.

A worksheet for a Positive Scenario

Domains	Potential high-impact, high-probability events (from base scenario)	Positive scenario— Assumptions from extrapolations
Finance	Probability of economic downturn Growing credit-worthiness (and profit) Building respect of suppliers and customers	No obvious bubbles or overheating, could be mild when it comes. Very low debt, actually getting calls offering loans. Suppliers expanding credit lines and improving delivery.
Location	Opportunities for better location(s) Lease deadline must be renewed or terminated.	Found an excellent location with very good terms. Landlord has offered remodeling and expansion if we renew.
Operations	Increasing sales Expanding markets	Quality control has improved relationships. Sales starting to grow to foreign countries, all on Letter of Credit terms.

Management	Gaining experience and sophistication in all areas.	Everyone, inside and out, has noticed the quality and devotion of management.
Marketing	Increasing production Need for multiple suppliers Quality control more important Logistics becoming more important	No more backorders! No returns or rejections! Potential customers are calling us!
People	Increased staff Standardize employee training Train for greater responsibility Increasing opportunities	Stable core staff. Contractors (bookkeeper, driver, sales reps) working smoothly.

Figure 12.1- A worksheet showing assumptions for a positive scenario

Below, in figure 12.2 are examples of positive extrapolations written out in worksheet form. These examples may seem a little vague, but we are exploring a ten-year period, so you will be working within the wide range of positive yet plausible futures. When you add assumptions about these domains to the major events that you expect to occur over the next ten years, you can see how the positive assumptions change the nature of the scenario.

STEEP Analysis

Now look at the *outside* forces that may impact your business over the next ten years, using the same format as you have with the domains in figure 12.2. Choose the most optimistic outlooks for each category of forces to be consistent with this positive scenario.

External forces	STEEP assumptions
Social	Substantial advancements in reducing poverty in some areas, but long term wars and religious conflicts are more violent and targeting civilians. Waves of immigrants are meeting resistance. Developed countries worry about loss of industrial jobs to AI.
Technological	Huge advances in medicine, biology, and medical tech, DNA. Substantial advances in energy, robotics, nanotech and artificial intelligence.
Ecological	Global warming—the climate seems to be changing as predicted. Rain patterns shifting, leaving forests dry for wildfires. Warmer air holds more moisture that increases rainfall and flooding.
Economic	Rising worldwide economy, but tariffs, trade wars, isolationism threaten to reverse many gains.
Political	Change seems to be everywhere. Some leaders seem unaware or uncaring about consequences, local or worldwide.

Figure 12.2 - STEEP categories with optimistic projections.

Of these projections, the changing world economy over the next ten years will probably have a direct impact on the future of your business, affecting both opportunities and finances.

Advances in technology will probably directly impact both you and your stakeholders— family, friends, coworkers, and organizations. Based on these projections, the impacts of the other categories will probably be more indirect.

You may see how this positive scenario will shape up. It will be optimistic but within plausible limits. As you lay out each of the scenarios, keep asking yourself questions about what the next ten years could bring, but keep the answers within plausibility. Dream, imagine, be creative, but stay within the limits of what could reasonably be expected to happen in your business over the next ten years.

With that in mind, look at a two-axis matrix (Figure 12.3), which diagrams two key forces in the future of your business.

The *value* of the two-axis matrix lies in the selection of the forces on each axis, so it is important to test multiple internal and external forces with the matrix in order to uncover the most interesting combinations and possibilities.

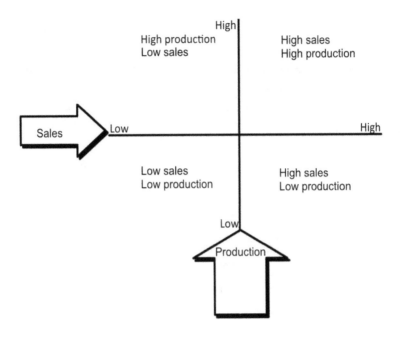

Figure 12.3- A two-axis matrix, offering a model for four plausible scenarios based on two internal forces, Sales and Production.

The two axis matrix shows a different story in each quadrant. Very brief stories, yet each quadrant can be the starting point for a plausible scenario. In this diagram, the best outcome is found in the upper-right quadrant.

Figure 12.3 shows "Sales" on the horizontal axis and "Production" on the vertical axis. In the upper left quadrant (High production, Low sales), imagine a manufacturing company with a machine that produces far more product each day than the business can sell. Changes in marketing might rebalance that problem, otherwise, the machine will frequently sit idle until demand catches up. The lower left quadrant (Low sales, Low production) offers a different challenge that could occur in almost any kind of business, from a single entrepreneur to a manufacturing business. The lower right quadrant (High sales, Low production) offers a challenging situation. Again, common in businesses of all sizes from a single professional, to a farmer or fishing boat owner to all sizes of manufacturing businesses. Tesla faced this problem in 2018 and successfully increased production dramatically.

In this example, the most desirable quadrant is at the upper right (High sales-High production).

A good place to start building a matrix for your business would start with the internal forces: Start with any force on one axis of the matrix and test that force against each of the others

Finances
Location
Operations
Management
Marketing
People

Next, consider some of the sub-forces in each of these categories, for example:

Profits	Leadership
Cash flow	Logistics
Building(s)	Distribution
Traffic	Advertising
Raw materials	Social media
Quality control	Wages and salaries
Growth	Taxes

Many of these sub-forces will also offer more components inviting you to continue to drill down.

The Negative Scenario

For the negative scenario, use the same basic information as in the first two scenarios. Now the projections for the domains will all be based on the worst plausible projections. Figure 12.4 shows some plausible projections. This takes you in a very different direction, to the lowest limits of plausibility as seen today. But this *is* plausible, and should be considered as a reasonable scenario, because the events are similar to those faced by millions of people in 2009.

Negative projections of Internal Forces

Domains	Potential high-impact, high-probability events (from base scenario)	Negative scenario— Assumptions from extrapolations
Finance	Probability of economic downturn. Growing credit-worthiness (and profit). Building respect of suppliers and customers.	Economic downturn Receivables not on time May have to borrow to meet payables.
Location	Opportunities for better location(s). Lease deadline- must be renewed or terminated.	Can't afford to move right now. Renew lease.
Operations	Increasing sales. Expanding markets.	Reducing staff.

Management	Gaining experience and sophistication in all areas.	Struggling.
Marketing	Increasing production. Need for multiple suppliers. Quality control more important. Logistics becoming more important.	Sales are down, not growing. Very stiff competition.
People	Increased staff. Standardize employee training. Train for greater responsibility. Increasing opportunities.	May have to lay off some employees.

Figure 12.4- Potential negative events.

Now add in negative assumptions for the world and the surrounding community (STEEP) to see a very challenging future if this scenario should actually occur. This illustrates why you need to create at least four different scenarios.

Assumptions

External forces	Negative STEEP assumptions
Social	Millions of people unemployed
Technological	Research and development slowing down
Ecological	Funds not available for cleanup projects
Economic	Worldwide economic downturn
Political	Great uncertainty Inadequate political response

Figure 12.5 STEEP categories with negative projections.

In the first three scenarios, you are putting boundaries around the future. You will have one scenario that extends the present into the future without major change, a second scenario that describes your best plausible future (top boundary), and a third scenario that describes the worst plausible future (bottom boundary). Your fourth scenario (wild card) will be outside those boundaries.

The Wild Card Scenario

Wild cards can be either positive or negative, but they will present a surprise. For the wild card scenario, forget about plausibility. Now you are talking about whatever may be *possible* in your business over the next ten years. You can make many versions of the wild card scenario, and you should make more than one.

You might start with a question. "What events or combinations of events could put your business out of business?" Set aside natural disasters for the moment and look at extreme economic events: best customer bankrupted without paying, bad cash flow management, legal events, employee, customer or competitor lawsuits, theft by a partner or employee, or failure by management to produce, read or understand financial reports.

Wild Card Events

Domains	Positive Wild Card scenario events	Negative Events that could put us out of business
Finance	No severe recession or downturn. Strong positive cash flow.	Inadequate capital. Theft. Slow or failed collection of receivables (cash flow).
Location	Site proves perfect for this business.	Fire, flood, hurricane or earthquake.
Operations	Products are very good quality. Excellent logistics.	Poor quality control.
Management	Management very aware of financials. Long term strategic plan .	Failure of management to monitor financials. Failure to anticipate change.
Marketing	Marketing plan and implementation proves successful.	Loss of major client.
People	Very conscientious and productive.	Major theft.

Figure 12.6 - Table showing two categories of possible wild card events.

The wild card worksheet shows high-impact, low-probability events within each domain that might happen. Each is possible, each would have a strong impact; none is very *likely* to occur. They provide a space for thinking about the futures that you do not expect—but *could* happen.

So now that you are looking beyond plausible futures, what are your *possible* futures? Will Earth be struck by an asteroid? Will global warming raise ocean levels and temperatures to a high level, or will nature reverse and turn to cooling and a new ice age? Will people live healthy lives of 150 to 200 years, or more? Will you be able to live forever inside a computer? These possible futures have been seriously suggested by knowledgeable people.

Some people take the ostrich approach to wild cards. They simply ignore them because they cannot deal with a future with no limits. So how do you put boundaries on the possible futures? Start with the possible futures that affect your business. Weigh the probabilities. Our definition of wild cards includes the phrases, "low probability" and "high probability". You will have to decide how low, or how high.

I mentioned earlier that one of my personal wild cards is hurricanes. Based on history, a hurricane may find me here in South Texas once in twenty to twenty-five years, a 4–5 percent risk. That is low probability, but it is a much higher probability than an asteroid strike. Like the business cycle, once a hurricane strikes, there may be a period of time before the next one lands. In my area of South Texas, the typical time between hurricanes may be twenty years. However, weather patterns are unpredictable, so we prepare for the possibility of a hurricane every year. Futurists consider the odds, but they are also alert to signals of change in the world.

In the next table, consider some possible, high-impact events that could occur in the world or in the community over the next ten years.

High Impact, High Probability Events

Domains	Potential high-impact, high-probability events (from base scenario)
Finance	Probability of economic downturn. Growing credit-worthiness (and profit). Building respect of suppliers and customers.
Location	Opportunities for better location(s). Lease deadline- must be renewed or terminated.
Operations	Increasing sales. Expanding markets.
Management	Gaining experience and sophistication in all areas.
Marketing	Increasing production. Need for multiple suppliers. Quality control more important. Logistics becoming more important.
People	Increased staff. Standardize employee training. Train for greater responsibility. Increasing opportunities.

Figure 12.7- Scenario categories with wild card possibilities.

Positive and Negative Possibilities

External forces	Wild card scenario. Positive and negative STEEP possibilities
Social	Revolution against extremism. Human Lifespan exceeds 120.
Technology	Cures or preventions for most major diseases. Solar becomes major source of energy. Auto industry abandons internal combustion engines. Worldwide Internet crash.
Ecology	Global warming accelerates. World responds to warming threat with drastic change and tech. Natural disasters increase in frequency and destruction (hurricanes, fires, tornados, earthquakes, floods, etc.).
Economic	Global currencies. Extreme inflation. "Farmed food" shortages open door for nutritious artificial foods.
Political	World religions work together to create world peace. Nuclear war.

Figure 12.8 - STEEP categories with wild card possibilities.

Sometimes it is tempting to select one event and build a scenario around it. This is okay, but events and forces tend to affect each other. One force may accelerate another force, as wind accelerates fire, while a different force, rain, could dampen and slow the fire. Any of the events shown in these two tables (Figures 12.7 and 12.8) could provide the change forces for a complete scenario. More efficiently, by placing two events into a two-axis matrix, you can set up some interesting wild card scenarios, as you will see a little later in this chapter. Futurists commonly test several forces against each other to see how the forces interact.

The Aspirational Scenario

The aspirational scenario is unique—this scenario is about choice and determination. Like the other scenarios, it is set on the same background of anticipated high-probability, high-impact events.

What are your aspirations for *your* business or profession? These could include one or more of the following:

- Build a many-person business that will provide you a good living for the rest of your life.
- Build a one-person business that will do the same.
- Build a business generating more than one-million dollars annual sales/revenues.
- Build a business generating more than x-million dollars annual sales/revenues.
- Build a business that allows you to travel widely.
- Build a business that provides unique services or products.
- Build a business that will make you extremely wealthy.
- Build a business that will allow you to be widely recognized, even a celebrity.
- Build a business based on your unique invention, device, or discovery.
- Build a product or service that helps many people in need.

You may choose any or many of these aspirations, or design something completely different. Then create a scenario about how you might achieve this scenario. Below (Figure 12.9) are some considerations in matrix format.

Possible Aspirations

Domains	Multi person organization	One-person organization
Finance	Personal capital plus bank loans as needed.	Personal capital, credit cards. Kickstarter if needed.
Location	Single location for all production, storage, shipping and receiving and customer access and service.	One room in home with computer, software, Internet, printer, phone.
Operations	Receiving, production, shipping by employees.	All logistics and services by contractors. Little or no inventory except samples.
Management	Partners, accountant, attorney.	Me!
Marketing	Local, national and/or worldwide.	Worldwide.
People	Staff, production workers, contractors, suppliers, and customers.	Suppliers, contractors, customers and potential customers.

Figure 12.9- A worksheet showing two approaches to an aspirational future. The multi-person business could include retail, wholesale, professional, or manufacturing businesses. The single person business could do almost anything.

Look at these goals from a different perspective using the futurists' traditional tool, the two-axis matrix.

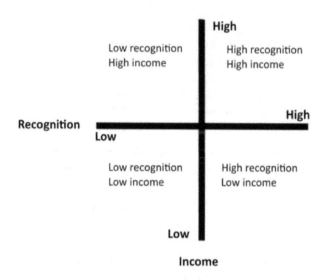

Figure 12.10- Two aspirations in a matrix, Recognition and Income. You can see that there is a story about a possible future in each of the four quadrants.

Here you can see personal or business recognition on the horizontal axis, and income on the vertical axis, offering several possibilities. In the upper left quadrant, the individual and the business receive low recognition and high income. For some people who appreciate privacy, this may be the preferred quadrant.

In the lower left quadrant, the business achieves neither high recognition nor high revenues. In the lower right quadrant, high recognition is received, but low income. The upper right quadrant offers both high income and high recognition.

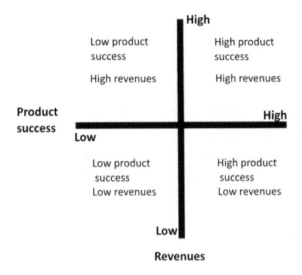

Figure 12.11- Two more aspirations in a matrix, this one weighing the success of a single product against revenues.

You may be wondering how a product in Figure 12.11 can have high revenues but low product success. One possibility is that the people who learned about the product paid a high price, but not many people were aware of the product. In the lower left quadrant, the product was unsuccessful, so revenues were low. The lower right quadrant suggests buyers loved the product, but wouldn't pay the price, although this could also be a case of high distribution costs. Finally, in the upper right quadrant, the product was successful and the business was rewarded with high revenues.

These examples are simple, but the two-matrix tool is very effective. The important thing about the matrix is the selection of forces on each of the two axes. You will have to try several forces and several combinations to get the best results.

Aspirational Scenario—Negative External Forces

External forces	External Events
Social	Discontent seems everywhere. No one seems to have quite enough.
Technological	Change is very slow. Many promising technologies just don't seem to get to the market place.
Ecological	Warming is increasing faster than expected. Needed technologies are not yet economic.
Economic	Economy is still very slow. Not enough jobs and too many over-qualified applicants.
Political	Promises, argument, and blame, but no positive change. Political brinkmanship risks war.

Figure 12.12- This looks like forces for a negative scenario, but in fact these are the forces that are in play as you develop an Aspirational scenario. The point is that anyone can aspire to an excellent future for their business, no matter what is happening in the surrounding world.

Examples Using the Two-axis Matrix

Here is another practical example of a two-axis matrix as an aid to decision making. In this case, you will look ahead to explore an exit strategy. Exiting your business can be an emotional process or a simple business decision. Planning for your exit several years in advance will help reduce the emotional impact.

A few exit choices include:

- Sell the business to another business or to an individual.
- Take the business public and sell shares of stock to the public.
- Pass the business on to family members.
- Close or liquidate the business.

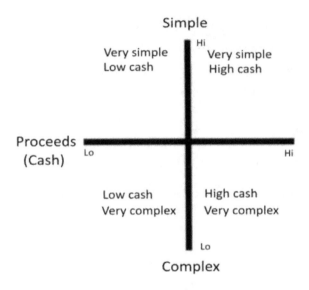

Figure 12.13 - This matrix shows four quadrants that result when the forces of cash meet the choices (or realities) of simplicity versus complexity.

In other words, do you want to maximize the cash or other benefits you will receive from selling your business? Do you want to minimize the complexity? Taking your business public is a long, complex process, but can be very rewarding. Closing or liquidating your business can be very simple, but you forfeit any value your business has as an operating enterprise. There is value in having a plan several years ahead of your expected exit. You can always change the plan if an unexpected opportunity arises.

You now have examples of five different types of scenarios that you can use as models to guide you as you develop your own scenarios.

- Continuation of the present scenario
- Positive or best plausible scenario
- Negative or worst plausible scenario
- Wild card scenario
- Aspirational scenario

With these models as a starting point, use the two-axis matrix to match any two forces you can imagine. As you practice this process, you will recognize that the matrix is a very powerful tool.

In the next chapter, you will create and write scenarios for your business.

CHAPTER 13

Telling Stories about the Future of Your Business

Concept

The act of writing scenarios reveals how forces and events interact, and how each scenario can develop over time.

I n this chapter, you will create and write scenarios, stories about the future of your business. I recommend that you actually write each scenario. These written scenarios don't have to be long, but you should write enough for each scenario so that it will make sense when you read it a year from now. When you re-read your scenarios, you will want to see what actually changed and what forces caused the change. If you write that much, you will be able to compare your scenarios with reality—what has actually happened in your business compared to what you wrote.

You should create and write at least four different scenarios:

- Continuation of the present into the future.
- Best plausible scenario.
- Worst plausible scenario.
- Wild card scenario.

183

In addition, if you have an aspiration for the future of your business, be sure to write that scenario in as much detail as you can. It will help you build your aspirational plan.

Beginnings

The quadrants in a two-axis matrix should suggest some good plots. It's worthwhile to think about the forces that will be at work in all aspects of your business, then put those forces into a matrix. Some of those will tell important stories, others will not. They will all help you think about how the forces in your business and how the forces in the world around you can impact and change your business.

The first lines of a scenario are sometimes the hardest to write. Here are a few examples of how you might start a scenario.

- I had known for years that I wanted to have my own business, but I didn't know what I wanted to do! I didn't want to own a restaurant, or a repair shop, or a retail store. Then I realized...

- Sometimes I ask myself, "How did I get to this point in my life?"

- Starting a small business scared me. I knew I could do it, but would it put my family at risk?

- After ten years in our own business my partners and I are amazed at what we've accomplished.

- When I was fired, it was the worst day of my life. Ten years later, I think it was the best day!

- When my partner proposed we start this business, I said there was no way we could get the funding together. She said, "Let's try!"

There are a few opening lines to get you started. From there, tell your story about starting and building your business as though you

184

were writing it from the future, *ten years from now*. Include information about the events and forces that you have considered for this scenario, then add your imagination, and write each scenario as though it was a chapter in the story of your business.

Structure

A little structure may help you get your story moving. Writers often say that a story must have a beginning, a middle and an end. That approach can give you a framework for an outline.

Opening sentence: When I was fired, it was the worst day of my life. Ten years later, I think it may have been the best!

Beginning: Where did you get the idea for your business? What did you have to do?

Middle: What happened over the decade? What forces impacted or changed your business? What events occurred along the way?

End: Where are you at the end of ten years? What do you see in the future?

As mentioned earlier, Journalists traditionally try to answer six questions in any story:

Who? What? When? Where? Why? and How? Not in any particular order.

For example, the "Who" may be you and any partners or family members you want to include.

You'll find that by the time you work through this framework and these questions you will have a story about the future of your business.

There are several values in creating these scenarios. First they will force you to think seriously about the future of your business and many of the events that could or should happen. You will also think seriously about the impacts of these events and possible ways to avoid negative events or encourage positive events. The scenarios will become "maps" to your potential futures, showing you where you are and where you could be. You can constantly compare your reality with your scenarios and identify which scenario you are in or headed toward in time to make adjustments if necessary.

Finally, you can always write new scenarios that are better aligned to the new realities of your business as the world changes around you.

Looking ahead

As you start looking ten years ahead, you will start recognizing forces and patterns in the world around you—in your business, in your community, and in your country and the world. Being aware of the forces of change as they move through your world can help you to anticipate the good changes and the troublesome changes. This anticipation, or foresight, reduces the number of surprise situations that may put you on the defensive, forcing you to react. Whenever you can anticipate events before they happen (before they become a problem) you have some control and usually time to think and prepare for whatever the situation may be.

Recognize what is important. There are many events in our businesses that are simply not important. Recognizing what is really important in your business will help you sleep better because you will not be worrying about things that do not make a difference. Sometimes, our reactions to unimportant events make a greater commotion than the events themselves. You may find it helpful when faced with a stressful situation to ask yourself "Is this really important? Will it make a difference a year from now?"

Use mini-scenarios to make decisions. When you face a decision, ask yourself, "What's the worst thing that can happen? What's the best thing that can happen? What could happen that would be a real surprise?" Ask again. Is that really the best? Really the worst? Now, you have a little more information to help you make your decision.

Use the two-axis matrix. You can draw this on a napkin, an envelope, your computer. Anywhere. While a graduate student, I once attended a meeting of professional futurists in which eight of us sat at a round table listening to the speaker. At some point, I realized that each person at the table had drawn a two axis matrix, showing the forces the speaker was describing. The matrix is a tool that can be used at any level. Just pick two forces and see where they could go in relation to each other. Practice with this tool and you will be surprised by the insights that you will develop.

Be aware of existing scenarios. Go to Google and search for "Scenarios about the future" and look through at least ten pages of results. Read some scenarios and understand them. Do you agree with them as plausible futures? Are they up to date? Do you see different scenarios? Visit www.shell.com and search for "Scenarios". Shell was an early developer of scenarios and scenario methods, leading the way for futurists and businesses worldwide. The Shell.com site usually features a number of scenarios about the future, and may include some of their classics from the past.

That sums up this section on anticipating change and exploring the future with scenarios. When you finish your scenarios, you will be ready to create or change the future of your business with strategic planning.

A Strategic Plan for Your Small Business

A strategic plan is just what the name suggests—a plan for the future based on strategies to achieve a future that you have envisioned.

This implies that in order to strategize and plan, you must first determine what future you want for your business—a vision. If you think about the future you want for your business ten years from now, what future do you see, or envision?

- **The first step** in your strategic plan will be to create *a vision of the future*—the future you choose or *prefer* for your business. For a ten year plan, the vision is what you want, what you plan, and what you will work to achieve over the next ten years.

- **Second,** do you have a mission for your business for this period? Something critical that must be achieved? Do you have goals or desires that you have not included in your vision? Now is the time to write all these things down in one place and get ready to plan to achieve or deal with your interests and concerns over this time period.

- **Third** in your strategic planning process is to *create strategies* that will help you achieve your goals and your vision of the future as well as deal with anticipated high impact events that may occur.

189

- **Fourth**, you will develop an *Action Plan*— a sequence of actions you will take each year, to execute each of your strategies. You will then analyze your plan looking for vulnerabilities and gaps.

- **Fifth**, you will devise *contingency plans* to deal with the wild cards that may occur during the next ten years. These are high impact events that are unlikely to occur, but if they do, you will have a contingency plan in place.

- **The final step** is to *experience the plan* you have created. Take the actions and follow the strategies you have selected to achieve your vision, but continue to monitor your plan, your business and the world around you. Has anything changed that affects your plan? If so, then adjust your plan to fit the new circumstances. Your strategic plan is a tool that you can use. It will help you achieve the future you want for your business.

CHAPTER 14

Strategic Planning for a Small Business

Concept

The strategic planning process is simple:

- Develop a *vision* of the future that you want to achieve over time.
- Develop *strategies* to achieve that vision.
- Develop a step-by-step, year by year *plan* for executing your strategies.
- Draw up a *contingency plan* to deal with low probability, high impact events.
- Follow the plan.

Strategic Planning Works

Strategic planning works! I sincerely believe that. Over the years, there has been criticism of the process, but most of that has faded. I find that strategic planning is now better understood and accepted.

Some of the difficulties with the strategic planning process had to do with the nature of large organizations. First, any large organization has multiple divisions, each with its own interests and agenda. The organization will also have individuals at all levels that have a personal interest in how a strategic plan might affect them. That means that there will be negotiations and jostling for advantage throughout the planning process. In order to arrive at agreements, there are often many compromises. Some of those disagreements may have been bruising disputes that are never forgotten. Finally, some strategic plans are just plans without strategies. This was more true twenty years ago when strategic planning was still new. Some planners simply neglected to develop strategies to achieve their plans. Finally, some strategic plans were never actually implemented. There are other reasons as well, but you get the idea. Size can sometimes be a disadvantage.

So in strategic planning, small may be good, as there are fewer decision makers, fewer influences, and fewer disputes. In your small business, the decision makers will usually be limited to a few people, or just one-person. That one factor makes a huge difference between small business planning and strategic planning in large organizations, including governments. As a result, strategic planning for a small business can be *very* effective. Even if your plan goes into a drawer and seldom comes out, once you have gone through the process, the plan is stored in your memory.

The Strategic Plan

What is a strategic plan, and how will you make one?

A strategic plan is a *long-term* plan, usually at least ten years, for the future of your business. Your plan will be based on research you have done in the previous sections of this book.

Start your strategic planning by deciding what you *want your business to be ten years from now.*

Next you will make strategies and plans to achieve that future, followed by actions you will take each year to make your plan and your vision a reality by the tenth year. To be more specific:

1. Think about and write down what you want your business to be in ten years. This is your *vision* of the future.
2. Create *strategies to achieve your vision* of the future and strategies to deal with the high-probability or high-impact events that may occur over the next ten years.
3. Create an *Action Plan*. This will be a schedule of actions that your business will take each year to implement your strategies, moving the business toward your vision of the future.
4. Create a *contingency plan*. This will be a plan to deal with the low-probability, high-impact events that might threaten to disrupt your business in the future.

That is your strategic plan in just four steps.

Even as you are creating your vision of the future, keep in mind that if you change your mind about what you want the future to be

193

for your business, you can change the vision and the plan. If your vision and plan no longer fit what you want from the future, change the vision and the plan.

How Strategic Planning Works

When you create a vision, you are defining what you *want* the future of your business to be. You are also identifying a destination—the place where you want your business to be ten years from now. Once you spell out where your business is going you can start making decisions about how to get there—how to reach your destination, your vision of the future. The strategies you choose will determine *how* you will get to the future and *how* you will deal with events along the way. That is why this is called strategic planning.

It is all as simple as thinking about what you *want* your business to be in ten years, and what you *have* to do over the next ten years to achieve that. Then you must develop specific strategies that will achieve that. In this way, you will achieve what you want and accomplish whatever you must. This is simply a matter of figuring things out in advance so that you know what you must do to actually achieve the future you want within ten years!

If you don't have a strategic plan, you might end up ten years from now with the same dream, the same vision for your business, but without having accomplished it.

Next, you will decide on the strategies you will use to take your business into the future, then lay out a timeline for each strategy. The timeline will tell you when to take each step forward and when to execute each strategy over the next ten years. Some strategies may take the whole ten years while other strategies may take a shorter time. Your Action Plan is like a ten-year calendar with all of your timelines spelled out so that you know when to take each step toward achieving your future.

If you accomplish each of the steps in each of your strategies within ten years, you should arrive at the future for which you have planned. That is how strategic planning works—and it does work.

Ask yourself one more time—what do you expect from the future? What is the future you *want* for your business ten years from now?

In the next chapter you will be exploring that question in order to build your vision, your destination in the future.

CHAPTER 15

A Vision of the Future for Your Business

Concept

In this book, a vision is an image, or mental picture, of your business at a time in the future, an image that you believe can be achieved. That image becomes a goal to be attained.

What Is a Vision?

How would you imagine or describe what your business will look like ten years from now? Think of one sentence that describes your image of what you *want* your business to be in ten years. The emphasis here is on your desired or *preferred* future.

A vision of the future may mean many things. For organizations conducting strategic planning, a vision is an image of the organization at some time in the future, usually ten to twenty years away. Working with the stages of business development, you can build mental images for each stage to help anticipate the future for your business. In this chapter, you learn how to create a vision for your business for the next ten years. That may cover several stages of your business.

At this point in your planning, you should be able to describe a clear vision for the next stage of your business, but what about the lifetime of your business? What would make you feel that your business and your efforts have ultimately succeeded?

A Vision is a Destination in the Future

If you plan a business trip or a family vacation, your first and most important decision is the destination. Where are you going?

Until you answer that question, you cannot make decisions about travel, where you will stay, or what you will do.

The same applies to your business—until you know where you want your business to go or be, it is difficult to make good decisions about the future of the business.

Start by looking at each of the major components of your business:

Finance- What do you want to see for the financial position of your business in the next ten years? Net worth? Sales? Debt? Profit? Growth rate? How much do you expect, or want your business to grow over the next ten years? What do you have to do to achieve that growth?

Location- Where do you want your business to be physically located in ten years? One location or multiple locations? One country or multiple countries? High traffic retail areas, industrial parks, office buildings, or an office in your home?

Operations- What will your operations look like? Professional services (medical, legal, accounting, religion, engineering, architectural, etc.)? Wholesale, distribution and warehousing?

Manufacturing? Transportation? Importing or exporting? Obviously, there are more types of businesses than I can list here, but a small business can be one-person at a desk, a few to dozen people, or many more. You know what your business operations are now, and you will have to decide what they can be ten years from now. What logistics will be required to deliver your products or services?

Management- Ten years from now, who will be on your management team? Will management be just you and your accountant, or will you have a board of directors? What will it take to build that team?

Marketing- How will you make potential clients/customers aware of your business? On line, offline, word of mouth, social media, advertising, sales force, direct mail/email campaigns? Will you advertise? How widely and what media? Will you automate (artificial intelligence)? Affiliates?

People- Ten years from now, how many people will be involved in your business as employees or contractors? Just you? Dozens? Hundred? Thousands?

Lots of questions, but your answers will help you build your vision of what you want or expect your business to be ten years from now.

Here's an example of a worksheet from the *Small Business Foresight Workbook*. You can create similar worksheets in any word processor, then fill in your vision of the future for each of the six domains in your business.

Sample Worksheet

Domain	Your Ten-year vision for each domain
Finances Sales, net worth, debt, collections, receivables, insurance, taxes.	More than $5 million in annual sales. No debt, receivables all current.
Location Primary office in home of owners(s)	Office in owner's home. High speed Internet service and Wi-Fi. Up to date computers, office equipment, and software. Temporary off site storage as and where needed.
Operations Research, development, purchasing, production, shipping	Monitor the quality of products and services. Update technology frequently. Develop new products and services.
Management Owners, advisors	Owners and professional advisors, (bookkeeper, CPA, attorney). Monitor new or improving technologies. Involve and train younger family member.
Marketing Sales, products, services, advertising, promotion	Steady growth in sales. Regularly introduce new product or service. Stay aware and ahead of the competition. Define and grow market areas nationally and internationally.

People Owners, suppliers, customers, and contractors/advisors	Owners and experienced professionals.

Figure 15.1- An example of a worksheet for developing a vision for a small business.

This simple worksheet is a start towards building a vision of your business over the next ten years. You should look at each part of your business and explore what needs to change over that time. If you increase sales over ten years, then you will have to increase your capability to produce products or services. Also look at what is changing outside of your business that impact you. Will changing technology such as artificial intelligence or robotics help you? Could you use a virtual assistant? Substantial changes and progress in those areas are already occurring, and may be an advantage for you, or for your competitors.

In addition to thinking about your vision for your business, take some time to look at the world around you. Look back at the notes or worksheets you have already created as you read previous chapters. What do you think is going to change over the next ten years that will have an impact on you and your business?

Will peace break out all over the world? Will there be a really big war? Will the world unify to reduce or reverse climate change? Will the impacts of poverty be reduced or eliminated? Will low-cost water be available to everyone? Will there be major breakthroughs in curing diseases and conditions? Will the human lifespan grow longer? What new technologies will emerge? What will be the impacts of new technologies? What opportunities are ahead for your business? In the next chapter, you will consider strategies to achieve your vision.

CHAPTER 16

Strategies to Achieve Your Vision

Concept

A strategy is a way to do something—but you must decide on which strategies are best for your business to achieve each component of your vision.

A Strategy is "How?"

How will you achieve your vision of the future for your business? By creating strategies that will achieve your goals or overcome any obstacles.

Do you already have strategies or plans to deal with change in your business?

When you created your vision for the future of your business, you made decisions as to what you wanted your business to be in ten years. Now, you are going to decide on how you can maneuver your business through the next ten years and which strategies you will use to achieve your goals.

If your business grows, that may mean more employees, more equipment, more space, more expense, and more income. How will you manage each?

What is your strategy to prepare for and deal with the next business downturn? The business cycle takes us through years of growth, then turns suddenly downward, damaging or destroying many businesses and individuals who are unprepared. How will you prepare for a downturn? What is your strategy?

If you are planning now for the next ten years, there is a good possibility that there will be a downturn or a crash during that time (Assuming you are not in the middle of a downturn now!) So, what are your strategies? Are you prepared to deal with a crash? I suggest you start with the six domains and ask yourself what preparations are necessary in each domain.

Here are two examples of strategies devised by a small business. Figure 16.1 suggests some strategies to achieve the ten-year vision of a very small (one-person) business.

One-person Business—Ten Year Strategy

Domains	Strategies to achieve your vision
Finances	**Keep tight controls on credit**: Sales to individuals or one-time purchases by credit or debit card or PayPal. Businesses on 30 day accounts based on credit application and credit approval with limits. Monitor receivables ruthlessly. Bookkeeper manages receivables and payables, accountant reviews monthly. Owner monitors cash flow and receivables.
Location	**Office at home.** One room with high-speed Internet service, workspace and storage space.
Operations	Products will be designed to be physically created and drop-shipped by contracted suppliers or created and delivered electronically. Computer, software, apps, printer, tablet and cell. Inventories will be maintained at practical operating levels.
Management	Single owner-operator, officer, with spouse. Incorporated as a subchapter S corporation. **Core strategy**: Keep business within what I can handle on my own with no employees.
Marketing	Marketing primarily from web site, social media, attendance and participation at professional conferences, and presentations to business and professional organizations.
People	One owner, designer, marketer. One contract bookkeeper, a CPA firm and an attorney.

Figure 16.1- Some strategies for a one-person business.

The next strategies focus on high impact events that could occur over the next ten years.

High Impact Strategies

Domains	Strategies to deal with high-impact events
Finances	To deal with a sudden cash flow problems, maintain a reserve, an available line of credit, personal savings or even credit cards.
Location	Retain a monitoring/alarm service to provide alerts and notify authorities to fires, break-ins, vandalism, etc. Be prepared to protect the building(s) from high winds and high water during hurricane season or fires during fire season in vulnerable areas.
Operations	Create spaces to store electronic or high value equipment above flooding. Back up EVERYTHING electronic, off premises and cloud.
Management	Anticipate any positive or negative situations. Make a list of possible crises. Stay on top of all areas of the business and be ready to respond quickly to any event.
Marketing	Be prepared to move quickly to deal with negative events or respond to positive events.
People	Prepare a plan to remove people from area well ahead of high risk weather, fire or other events that give any warning. Listen carefully to employee concerns and suggestions. Provide first aid kits, emergency numbers and a plan to deal with injuries or emergencies.

Figure 16.2 Strategies for a small business of any size.

Strategies can sometimes get complex, and it may be helpful to go back to basics and remember simple strategies.

Some Simple Strategies

Sometimes simple is the best solution.

Domains	Some Simple Long Term Strategies
Finances	Don't lose money! Keep excellent financial records, IRS filings, legal documents.
Location	Protect your property! Maintain buildings, signs, and sites in good condition and appearance. Make any repairs immediately. (see broken window theory- https://en.wikipedia.org/wiki/Broken-windows_theory)
Operations	Keep everything running smoothly! Keep all equipment maintained and raw materials in clean condition. Finished goods ready to ship.
Management	Know what's happening! Management should be fully informed and updated on status and any situation.
Marketing	Take care of your customers! Find new business! Aggressively search and research new market areas and new products.
People	Take care of your people! Keep people at all levels fully trained and cross trained.

Figure 16.3- Long term strategies that will apply through all stages of the business including the exit stage.

These may be simple strategies, but they are a place to start. Having a strategy in mind to deal with challenging situations will give you a head start on many other businesses.

Building a strategy

A common question from small business owners is, "How do I grow my business?".

One answer is to look at the basics and ask the same questions— Who? What? When? Where? Why? and How? So going back to the question, "How do I grow my business?" You could ask yourself the following questions:

Who are logical buyers for my products and services?

What do buyers need from my business that I can provide?

When do they need my products or services? Is demand seasonal? All year long? Specific needs?

Where are my present and potential customers? On the Internet? In my community or country? Where can I actually deliver my products or services?

Why are potential customers not buying from me now?

How can I reach my potential customers?

The answers to those questions will be the beginnings of strategy development. For example, start with a "Why?" question— "Why are current customers buying from me now?" If you don't know the answer, ask them! Common answers would include:

1-They know and like the product or service.

2-Friends have recommended you or your business.

3-They have heard about your business several times.

With real answers, you can develop strategies. Some possible strategies might include:

- Ask customers to write testimonials that may encourage potential customers or clients.
- Ask customers to recommend your business to their friends, possibly offering a bonus, coupons, or discounts.
- Publicize and/or advertise your business through traditional (print, radio, TV, mail, signage) media and social media.

This example of strategy is simplistic, but these methods are used around the world to help grow businesses of all sizes. You can learn a great deal about strategy by studying how other businesses have successfully applied strategies to achieve success.

In the next chapter you will develop an Action Plan that will guide your business into the future by putting your strategies into action.

CHAPTER 17

Creating an Action Plan

Concept

Once you have created strategies, you must decide when to use them and in what sequence. The Action Plan develops the sequence in which each strategy is applied, mapping the strategies and the actions over the time period you establish for the plan. Some strategies may be executed immediately while other strategies may take the entire time period of the Action Plan.

An Action Plan is "When"

This chapter is where you turn your strategies into actions. First, develop a sequence of actions, then create a schedule. What actions must you take, starting today, to achieve your vision of the future? What is the best sequence for those actions? *When* will you act?

These are the actions that can change your business, but until you actually take action, nothing in your planning will change the future.

The Action Plan is the central document of your strategic plan. You can (and should) modify or change your plan as you go along, because events will not unfold according to plan, so stay flexible, but keep working toward your preferred future.

Strategies and Sequences

Your Action Plan is about identifying each of the strategies that you expect to put into action over the next ten years, then organizing those strategies into a sequence of actions. In many cases, you will need to complete one strategy before you can start on the next.

For example, if you decide to launch a marketing campaign in a major city next year, you may need to set up logistics in that city before you actually start your marketing campaign. In brief, your sequence might be:

1. Arrange warehouse space and services.
2. Arrange shipping and delivery services from this new location
3. Place inventory in the new warehouse.
4. Start new marketing campaign.

You won't need that much detail in your ten-year Action Plan, but this demonstrates the value of a sequence of actions.

For a one-person business, a list of strategies for the next ten years might look like the following.

Micro Business Strategies

Domains	Strategies for the next ten years (For a Micro Business)
Finances	Protect cash! No risks! Resist borrowing. Buy on 30 day terms. Sell on cash/credit card terms.
Location	At home.
Operations	Design products, contract for manufacturing and shipping on demand. Keep adding new products!
Management	Spouse and me. Convert to S Corporation (U.S.).
Marketing	Build active Web site, offer free content. Respond to visitor signups. Social media with ads-Google and Facebook Write regular blog, magazine articles. Build email lists-customers, inquiries, visitors.
People	Contract bookkeeper, attorney. Suppliers. Buyers. Sales agents.

Figure 17.1- A few strategies for a one-person business. Very brief, but provides a list to guide the business into the future.

One of the attractions of very small or one-person businesses is the combination of simplicity, flexibility, control and total responsibility.

Completing the Action Plan

The blank Action Plan on the next page will hold a 10 year overview of your business that can be easily be expanded or recreated in a spreadsheet. Much of the information in your Action Plan will be taken from your Vision worksheet and various strategy worksheets.

Action Plan Worksheet

Vision/Goal (Ten Year)	Strategies (How)	Actions (To Do)	Timeline (When)
Finance			
Location			
Marketing			
Operations			
Management			
People			

Figure 17.2- A blank Action Plan worksheet, from the *Small Business Foresight Workbook*. Completed, this form will hold a 10 year overview of your business.

A multi-page example of how you might complete an Action Plan for your business for the next ten years.

Action Plan Example

Vision/Goal (10 Year)	Strategies (How)	Actions (To Do)	Timeline (When)
Finance More than $5 million in annual sales. No debt, receivables all current.	Protect cash. No risks! Resist borrowing. Buy on 30 day terms. Sell on cash/credit card. 30 day terms to regular clients.	Don't lose money. Keep excellent financial records, IRS filings, and legal documents.	Evaluate every year.
Location Office in home. Accessible to clients, visitors.	Office in home. Temporary warehousing as and where needed.		Year 5 evaluate.

Management Owners and professional advisors, (bookkeeper, CPA, attorney). Monitor new or improving technologies. Involve and train younger family member.	Spouse and me. Convert to S Corp. (U.S.). Create a retirement plan.	Know what's happening! Management should be fully informed and updated on status and any situation.	Year 2 convert to sub chapter S (US) corporation. Year 3 Create retirement plan. Year 5 Involve younger family member and train for future. Year 9 Evaluate and start new plan.
Marketing Steady growth in sales. Regularly introduce new product or service. Stay aware and ahead of the competition. Define and grow market areas nationally and internationally.	Quality products. Professional services. Participate in Industry conventions and conferences. Web site. Blog. Social media.	Take good care of customers! Find new business! Aggressively search and research new market areas and new products.	Year 2 Intro new product. Year 4 Intro new product. Year 6 Intro new product. Year 8 Intro new product. Year10 Intro new product.

Operations Develop new products and services. Monitor the quality of products and services. Update technology frequently.	Design products, contract for manufacturing and shipping on demand. Keep adding new products.	Keep everything running smoothly! Keep all equipment maintained and in clean condition. Finished goods ready to ship.	Year 1 develop new product. Year 3 develop new product. Year 5 develop new product. Year 7 develop new product . Year 9 develop new product.
People Owners, suppliers, customers, contractors and advisors.	Owners and experienced professionals.		Year 5 Introduce young family member into business.

Figure 17.3- An example of how a small business might document a ten year Action Plan. Your Action Plan will probably be longer and more complex than this example.

Note that the first column (Vision/Goal) is about your overall goals for the next ten years. The second column (Strategies) focuses on the strategies you expect to use to achieve those goals. The third column (Actions) describes the actions you expect to take to carry out your strategies, and the fourth column (Timeline) shows when you expect to execute your individual strategies.

Creating your Action Plan will take some time and will require you to think seriously about the future of your business. This chapter brings everything you've learned about using foresight tools and methods together. The completed Action Plan should be like a road map to the future of your business. From here, you can follow your map, make changes as you go, but you will always know where you are and where you are going.

Backcasting

Building a sequence of actions to be taken over the next ten years can be challenging, especially in the later years. Most of us find it easy to see a sequence of actions for several years ahead, but it gets harder. Futurists also had difficulty with Action Plans until someone came up with a clever idea. Start at the end of ten years and work backward!

The concept is simple—imagine or visualize what your business looks like ten years from now, having achieved your vision for the company's future.

- In your image of the ten-year future of your business, imagine as much detail as possible..
- What was the *last* action you had to take to achieve your vision?
- What was the action you took before that?
- And before that?

In other words, start at the end of the ten year period and work backwards to the beginning: Backcasting. It's a simple tool—and it works!

For example, look at Figure 17.3. You can start anywhere, but your plan says that the Marketing area is planning to introduce a new product in the tenth year, probably the same product that Operations plans to develop in year 9.

What is the very last thing that Marketing must do to complete your ten year strategic plan?

What was the next to last action, and the action before that? What must be done in each area of your business to complete your plan, and what was the action before that?

Figure 17.4 demonstrates (very briefly) how Backcasting can help you develop your Action Plan.

Backcasting Actions

Years in future	Actions taken to achieve your vision
Ten years in future	Introduced newest product. Reviewed financials and investments.
Nine years in future	Developed our newest product/service. Started on the next 10 year Vision, Strategies and Action Plan.
Eight years in future	Introduced newest product. Added another young family member to the business. Business is highly automated.
Seven years in future	Developed new product. Expanded warehousing and logistics. Create investment plan.
Six years in future	Introduced newest product. Overhaul technology.
Five years in future	Added young family member to business She's the future! Developed new product. Evaluated home office and decided to continue.

Four years in future	Introduced newest product. Warehousing products in multiple locations. Updated virtual assistance.
Three years in future	Developed new product. Created a retirement plan. Reviewed all financials and updated plan.
Two years in future	Introduced our newest product. Filed for Sub-chapter S corp.
One year in future	Developed and introduced our new product. Opened web site, started blog and social media.

Figure 17.4- Backcasting can help build the sequence of actions necessary for your Action Plan by working backward from the future. You may not need Backcasting if your plan has already come together, but it is a useful tool when you are sorting out the sequences and the actions you need to take.

Summarizing

Since you started this book, you have learned about the tools and methods that futurists use to anticipate the future, and you have learned how to use those tools and methods.

You have learned about plausible, ambitious, and wild card scenarios. You have learned how to create a vision of the future for your business then develop strategies to achieve that vision.

Finally, you have designed an Action Plan to the future for your business.

Completing your Action Plan should give you a great sense of accomplishment. You now have a roadmap to the future for your business. But, there is still a little more to do—you need to check your work!

In the next chapter, you will analyze your Action Plan using two very effective tools, Vulnerability analysis and Gap analysis.

CHAPTER 18

Analyzing Your Plan

Concept

It is always a good idea to review your work. Several tools from strategic planning are available to help you analyze your plan and strengthen it.

Vulnerability Analysis

What could threaten the financial position of your business? Could that threat bring down your company?

Once you have created a ten-year or longer plan for your business, think of your business as a table with six legs, each leg representing one domain of your business. If one leg collapses, will the other five hold the business up? Or would the collapse of one leg cause others to fail? What are the risks and what can you do to strengthen each leg?

Look at the six-legged table shown here. Now, ask yourself —for each leg, "Is this leg vulnerable now? What could cause it to become vulnerable in the future?"

To carry the thought further, what could cause any leg to weaken or collapse? What would be the impact on your business if one or more of the legs (domains) failed?

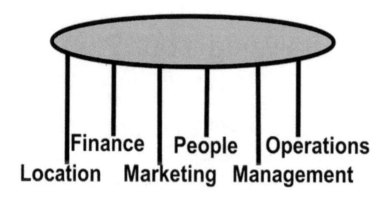

Figure 18.1- The six domains representing the forces of change within your business can each be an area of vulnerability.

Start with the Finance domain. What factors could collapse the financial side of your business, now or in the future? Slow receivables? Slow paying customers? Dependence on one or two customers for timely payment? Inadequate capital reserves? Too much cash drawn out by owners? Too much debt or debt expense? Employee fraud?

If you don't have any of these problems now, how can you protect your business against any of them happening in the future? For example, what financial controls do you have in place? Do the owners understand and review all financial report and details?

A Personal experience

Years ago, a friend with whom I had done business for several years started a new business. He invested in several large machines that cut very large rolls of paper into smaller widths or

---

cut them into sheets for printing. The business was successful from the day it opened. Sam was well known and well liked and he produced high quality products.

It looked like a perfect small business, but suddenly it was closed by the Internal Revenue Service because Sam had not paid his taxes! He protested that he had personally signed the checks to the IRS.

It turned out that Sam's bookkeeper had presented weekly batches of checks for Sam to sign. Apparently, Sam did not look carefully at each check, or at bank statements. The bookkeeper either made the checks out to herself, or altered the checks intended for the IRS and deposited them in her own account. Sam found little help from the legal system. It cost my friend his business and his home.

The vulnerability in this situation appears at first to be in the People domain and/or the Finance domain, but was in fact the responsibility of Management. Management makes the rules for how the business is run, including financial controls. In this example, one-person, the bookkeeper, was given responsibility (and control) for everything related to money in the business (not uncommon in small businesses). In this case, one solution might have been a fidelity bond, insuring the business against dishonesty by the bookkeeper. The bonding process could have revealed similar problems in the bookkeeper's past, and she would not have been hired. Other solutions would have been to hire a controller or contract for accounting services that would oversee the bookkeeper's work. But, the simple fact is that Sam trusted one-person and gave her complete responsibility and authority over the office and financials without adequate supervision or safeguards.

The above is an example of how one leg (of your business) collapsing can bring down the whole table.

It's important to look at each leg of this table frequently, and ask, "Where are we vulnerable, and what can we do about it?" The Finance area is obvious, but what about the other legs—what could become a problem?

Finance Do you have professionals (CPA, attorney, banker, insurance agent) monitoring and advising you on various aspects of the business' finances?

Location Is your business vulnerable to storms, fire, flooding, power outages? Is access limited to a single street or road? Will your lease be up for renewal soon? Is the business located in a high crime area?

Marketing Are any of your products or services subject to serious competition? Is there new technology on the horizon (Robotics, Artificial Intelligence) that could make your products or services obsolete?

Operations In many small businesses, a breakdown in one machine such as a forklift, an electric motor or pump, a computer (or system) can stop a portion of the business for one or several days. Do you have a backup or work-around? Do you rely on a single supplier for timely delivery of raw materials, components or critical supplies? If so, is an alternate supplier available?

Management Are you, your partners and managers growing your capabilities as quickly as your business is growing? Will anyone in management retire soon?

People Could one individual or a group disrupt the organization? Could a partner? Is anyone at particular risk for divorce, injury or death? Is anyone in a position to divert funds?

This chapter is about vulnerability, so we're exploring all the dark corners, but the truth is that if you leave openings, someone will take advantage.

In the next section we will look for gaps in your plan.

Gap Analysis

Gap analysis is the process of identifying desired outcomes, then comparing those with actual outcomes to identify the 'gap' between. If a production line is expected to complete 200 products per day, but is only averaging 150 units per day, the gap is 50 units per day. If your marketing plan is built on a sales forecast, and your sales are only on track for half of the forecast, then some action must be taken to close the gap. Increasing sales is the obvious choice, but if that is not possible, the next option may be to reduce production and spending. As mentioned earlier, Tesla was faced with a similar problem in 2018. They were not able to produce enough cars every day to meet their commitments. Management recognized the problem, took aggressive action, and succeeded in dramatically raising production levels.

This concept of gap analysis may be applied to all areas of the business, from defining employee skills, production levels, quality control standards, profits and losses, and management capabilities.

Once gaps are identified, the question is "How can the gaps be closed"? Tesla's solution was to quickly add a third assembly line, which, while appearing radical, worked.

In the case of your business plan, are your expectations too high or too low? When will you know? How often and when will you adjust your plan to close the gaps?

Gap Analysis in a Small Business

Domain	Plan	Potential Gap	Possible Solution
Finances	Receivables agreed 30 days.	Large customer slow 45-60 days.	Discuss/negotiate. Reduce credit line?
Location	Expand production space.	Building size is at maximum.	Add a floor. Add a location. New building.
Operations	Increase production.	Not enough space.	Expand building.
Management	Partner due to retire.	Wants 5 more years as active partner. Not pulling weight.	Negotiate exit. Add a person with needed skills to management.
Marketing	Expand marketing area.	Not enough production capacity.	Add production facility. Limit new growth.
People	Increase production staff.	Not enough space to expand production.	New location. Additional location. Scale back.

Figure 18.2- An example worksheet to help identify and deal with gaps in your business.

This worksheet should raise concerns. In Finances, a large customer is exceeding the thirty-day terms. Management (this could be you) will have to decide how important this is to cash flow, and what can or should be done about it. If the seller has more business than he can easily supply, then it is time to reduce the supply to this customer, but consider how that customer

Might respond or retaliate. In other areas, it appears that the business is having trouble meeting total demand for product and is are limited by the size of the present location. Again, management will have to make decisions about pricing, temporary production off site, and permanent new or additional production space.

This example demonstrates the advantage of identifying gaps that spotlight specific needs or problems. Finding gaps early gives you time to deal with a problem before it becomes a crisis.

This is a good point to go to your own business plan to analyze the plan for gaps. Look at each strategy, each goal or objective. Are they achievable with your present funding, facilities and personnel? Are there any gaps between your plan and your resources and abilities?

Unintended Consequences

Futurists are wary of unintended consequences, because there are consequences whenever changes are made. Most businesses plan for good consequences, but sometimes there are surprises, and some of those are not good. As a result, you should search for the unexpected or unintended consequences. Unintended consequences may result from nearly any kind of change.

Here are a few examples.

Unintended Consequences

Domain	Action	Consequence
Finances	You extend more credit to a customer who offers to buy a lot of your product.	The new customer buys a lot of your product, then goes bankrupt!
Location	Production area enlarged.	Expansion eliminated several employee and customer parking places.
Operations	You invest in new technology to speed up production. To increase production, you add a night shift.	The new system is fast, but has a lot of down time. Night shift has higher cost and lower productivity.
Management	Your business is growing so you add two new people to your Board.	Your new Board members want to change everything!
Marketing	Demand for your products encourages you to raise prices.	A competitor offers lower prices your customers.
People	You hire a new worker because he or she *needs* a job.	The new worker is not willing or able to be a good worker.

Figure 18.3- A few examples of unintended consequences.

In your business you will find situations or occasions that will produce results that are the opposite of what you intended. Very often, unintended consequences are simply the result of change, and there is a helpful answer for most situations.

The best advice I can offer is to think things through before you act.

In the next chapter you will explore Wild Cards and the values of Contingency Planning.

CHAPTER 19

Wild Cards and Contingency Plans

Concept

Sometimes the "unexpected" happens!

What happens if one of your wild card scenarios occurs? Or a "worst plausible" event unfolds?

You can develop contingency plans to deal with some of them. "If...then" strategies are also helpful for contingency planning.

A little further along, use the strategy column in Figure 19.3 to identify your general approach to dealing with this wild card or low probability event. Will you try to minimize, maximize, profit, or avoid loss? Consider all the low-probability, high-impact events you listed, including internal and external events.

Give each of these events serious attention. They may never occur, but if an event does happen, you'll be prepared with a contingency plan.

Wild Cards

Domain	Negative events	Positive Events
Finances	Failure of a major customer.	Saved by emergency reserve account! All receivables on time. Very high profitability.
Location	Business destroyed by fire, flood, earthquake or other disaster. City raises taxes.	City upgrades streets and lighting.
Operations	Loss of a major supplier.	Training program working! Quality control wins praise.
Management	Management takes a big chance and loses! Loss of a partner.	Management takes a big chance, and wins!
Marketing	Loss of major customer.	Gained a major customer or contract. Successful sales campaign.
People	Strike! Everyone has the flu!	Employees exceed all expectations!

Figure 19.1- Positive and negative wild cards to help you consider possible future events.

Wild cards are events that you don't expect to happen, but could. You should have a plan to deal with them if they occur.

Contingency Plans

Domain	Potential High impact event	Contingency plan: Actions
Finances	Growth may exceed cash flow.	Manage cash carefully Plan now to qualify with potential lenders. Build up reserves.
Location	May outgrow present location.	Search for alternate space or services.
Operations	Products being returned for poor quality.	Set up quality standards and controls.
Management	Business may not succeed	Fail fast!
Marketing	Demand may exceed our ability to supply!	Explore temp production space/staff.
People	People are quitting!	Find out why! Make corrections. Evaluate hiring and training standards.

Figure 19.2- Examples of potential high impact events and a few possible solutions.

This is the place to think about your fears! What potential events in your business would keep you up at night?

A Personal Experience

A new customer came to me, asking for packaging design and assembly.

I gave him quotes, terms and timelines. We worked together for several months. His payments were on time and he was very happy with the services I had provided. One month, his payment was late and I called him.

"I'll be in Saturday with a check." Friday morning he declared bankruptcy!

Within minutes of hearing, I called my attorney. Bill was a fraternity brother from college days and my contingency plan for legal problems. His response to my problem was brief and simple. "File a mechanic's lien *today*!"

Because I had supplied labor to assemble and package the customer's devices, I was able to file a mechanic's lien immediately, and recovered my entire bill in bankruptcy court, ahead of other creditors.

Aggressive, quick action, and knowing where to get good advice made the difference!

Make a list of the things about your business that worry you now or may trouble you in the future. Ask yourself how you might deal with those problems, or avoid them. Below are examples of strategies and plans for specific risks.

Worst Plausible Events

Wild card or Worst Plausible event	Strategy (how will we deal with this event?)	Plan (what actions will we take to deal with this?)
Hurricane	Prepare for evacuation, high water, high winds.	Transportation: vehicles and route to safety. Window covers. Plan to move electronic or fragile equipment to high place.
Earthquake	Strengthen building. Locate/strengt hen equipment to reduce risk.	Plan for evacuation.
Business cycle downturn	Have plan and funds to acquire weak competitors	Arrange time off for those who can use it. Plan to upgrade facilities. Hold cross training sessions.
Fire **Internal and External**	Call 911. Evacuate building. Evacuate area.	Install and maintain detectors/alarms in building. Eliminate clutter, maintain clear passage. Assign responsibilities. Set up system so everyone is accounted for. Confirm everyone has transportation from the area.

237

VERNE WHEELWRIGHT

Business is failing and no solution available	Fail fast! Stop your losses.	Don't panic—think it through. Strategize and plan, then execute. Stop buying. Terminate everyone who is not needed to close the business. Sell everything. Cancel or legally get out of all commitments.

Figure 19.3- An example of a simple plan for dealing with high impact events that you don't want to occur in your business.

These examples are all pretty obvious, but they are also events that happen to businesses every year, all over the world. Consider these risks before you commit to a business location.

What other risks can you anticipate?

If you are already committed to a location, what can you do to reduce or avoid these or other risks? How can you prepare for or deal with epidemics or angry people with guns?

Some of these "Worst Plausible" events seem very unlikely, but if you try to think of all the possibilities, you will have reduced the risks to yourself and your business. It is very easy to put off or ignore wild card events or low probability events, yet every day, unlikely events occur somewhere in the world. Fires, floods, mass shootings, earthquakes, tidal waves, terrorist attacks, explosions, and many more. If you take the time to consider the possibilities and how you might prevent or respond to some of these events, you will have taken another step towards preparing for the future.

238

In the next chapter you will put your plan into action and start working and living with your plan, tweaking it wherever necessary.

CHAPTER 20

Living with Your Plan

Concept

The concept is simple— make a plan, follow the plan, and change the plan as soon as you find it necessary or to your advantage.

You have now explored your business's present and future, created four or more future scenarios, designed a preferred future, devised strategies to achieve that preferred future and developed an Action Plan to take your business to that future. You have also considered contingencies and wild cards.

With all that, you should still be prepared to make adjustments to your plan whenever they becomes necessary.

Congratulations!

The next, most important step is very simple: Start following your Action Plan and working toward the future you have chosen for your business. Enjoy the benefits of your plan!

Live your plan!

After you have completed the plan for the future of your business, wait two weeks or more, then review your plan. You accomplished a lot by completing all of this. Now reflect on what

you have done and decide what you can do to improve your plan. Reevaluate your strategies, your Action Plan and your contingency plan. Redefine your vision. What did you leave out? What do you want to change? Go ahead. Make changes and improvements. This is *your* plan.

Make a note to yourself—in six months or a year, look over your plan again. What has changed in your business that affects your plan? What outside forces are affecting your plan? Are you making progress? Is a different scenario unfolding than you expected? Adjust your plan as necessary to deal with the changes, but keep moving toward your vision. You can even change or re-define your vision.

Monitor the changes in your business and the world each year, and keep reviewing and adjusting your plan whenever you feel it is necessary. If no changes are needed, then just keep following your plan.

Repeat this review every six months, or a year at the most. Keep checking to see that your plan is on track with reality

Also, keep your contingency plans up to date and be prepared to take action whenever necessary. If the risks of fires, floods or very bad weather are increasing, adjust your plan and take any actions that are appropriate as soon as you see the need. What new risks exist that you have not considered or planned for? Look closer, then write a contingency plan for each.

In short, maintain your plan, and keep extending it so you are always looking and planning ten years ahead.

When Your Vision Changes …

When your vision changes— change your plan! It really is that simple. Don't forget that this is your plan for your business. You wrote it, and you can change it.

If the world around you is changing, adjust your plan. If the business cycle turns down sharply, adjust your plan and start working toward the new reality of the future. If the economy soars, you may have to adjust your plan to the new realities.

> **A Personal Experience**
>
> In 2007, my vision of the future changed. I had planned to retire my business in 2010, but was very aware that if I had cargoes in ocean containers or even at their destination when the business cycle turned down, buyers would demand that I accept substantially lower prices to meet the new realities of the marketplace. I stopped accepting new orders, collected all receivables and retired before the crash. Just barely!
> My vision had changed and I exercised one of my contingency plans.

In the next chapter, we will look once again at the values of a long term perspective.

CHAPTER 21

The Long-Term Perspective

Concept

Whether you've simply skimmed this book or completely absorbed it along with the workbook, you've been exposed to some important concepts and ideas about preparing your business for the future.

Scalability Works for You

You have learned about a number of methods and tools used by professional futurists in businesses and governments around the world. In addition, you have learned how to apply these methods and tools in a small business—including a one-person business. More, you have learned that the methods are not only scalable, they can be used anywhere in the world.

Note that scalability works both ways. The methods in this book have emphasized smaller scale forces that are most important in a small business. As your business grows, these methods will scale up. You will find yourself working more closely with the STEEP forces as your experience increases and others take over the routines of the business.

The Long-Term Perspective

The ability to see events with a long-term perspective is a valuable trait. According to researchers James Kouzes and Barry Posner, having a long term perspective is second only to honesty in sought-after leadership traits.

Long term perspective is what this book is about—helping you to develop the skills to lead your business into the long term future.

Start simply. When faced with a decision, ask yourself, "What could happen? What is the worst case? What is the best case?" When you have good answers to those questions, you have put brackets around the future for that decision. You have narrowed the outcome to those outcomes that are plausible. That should help you with your decision.

Watch for the forces of change, internally and externally. Ask yourself questions, then find the answers. What is changing? What is causing that change? What is the driving force? How fast will it change? How far will this change go? Who will this change impact and how? To question a change, use the traditional questions that journalists have been asking since the beginning of journalism:

- Who?
- What?
- When?
- Where?
- Why?
- How?

Then ask yourself what this change will look like in ten years or longer.

That probably sounds too simple, and it may be. The key step (not mentioned above) is taking the time after asking the questions to develop and analyze the answers. In our fast-paced multi-tasking world, that may well be the key to learning about the future— taking the time to think about it.

In addition to acquiring a long term perspective for your business and for your own use, you may find value in helping others to acquire a long term view in their lives and their careers. If you are a parent, your children will benefit from realizing that teen years and time spent gaining an education are a very small part of a life that may exceed 100 years. For educators, helping students gain a perspective of time and the impact of an education on one's long term future may encourage more students to stay in school. For organizations of any type or size, there is clearly value in educating personnel at *all* levels in long term thinking.

Above all else, this book is about the future for you and your business. You now have the methods, the tools and the knowledge to make a good future for your business and for yourself!

References

This section provides references that are mentioned within the chapters. It also lists many of the authors and publications that influenced my writing of these chapters. In most cases the references will provide more detail on the methods or concepts described in the chapter.

Chapter 1 Small Business and the Future

Bell, Wendell. "Foundations of Futures Studies: Human Science for a New Era." New Brunswick: Transaction Publishers, 1997.

Cornish, Edward. Futuring: *The Exploration of the Future*. Bethesda: World Future Society, 2004.

De Geus, Arie. P. "Planning as Learning." Harvard Business Review, March-April (1988): 70-74.

Hines, Andy and Bishop, Peter, ed. *Thinking About the Future*. Washington, DC: Social Technologies, 2006.

Small Business.com (2018). "What is a 'Nonemployer Business?'" https://smallbusiness.com/employees/nonemployees

Chapter 2 Stages of Business Development

Gladwell, Malcolm, *The Tipping Point*, New York: Little Brown and Company. 2002.

"Athena" at Shaping Tomorrow, "Trend Alert 2019", 17 January, 2019. htpps://www.shapingtomorrow.com.

Malone, Thomas W. et al, "Do Some Business Models Perform Better than Others?" (May 2006). MIT Sloan Research Paper No. 4615-06. Available at SSRN:

Chapter 3 Stakeholders in Your Business
Churchill, Neil and Lewis, Virginia L.(1983) "The Five Stages of Small Business Growth." Harvard Business Review May, 1983. https://ssrn.com/abstract=920667.
Mintzburg, Henry; Ahlstrand, Bruce; Lampel, Joseph(1998). *Strategy Safari.* New York, Free Press, 1998.
Wheelwright, Verne. *The Personal Futures Workbook.* Harlingen: Personal Futures Network, www.personalfutures.net. 2008.

Chapter 4 Trends and Forces: Anticipating Change
Penn, Mark J. *Microtrnds.* New York: Hatchett Book Group, 2007.
Naisbitt, John. *Megatrends.* New York: Little Brown and Company,1984
Schwartz, Peter. *The Art of the Long View.* New York: Currency Doubleday, 1991.
Powers, Devon. *On Trends:* Champaign: University of Illinois Press, 2019.

Chapter 5 Forces in Your Business: Past, Present and Future
Taylor, Charles W. "Creating Strategic Visions" Futures Research Quarterly, Winter, (1991): 21-37.
Liedtka, Jeanne and Ogilvie, Tim. *Designing for Growth.* Chichester: Columbia University Press, 2011.
Cramer, James and Simpson, Scott. *How Firms Succeed 5.0.* Norcross: Greenway Communications, 2014.
Chapter 6- Forces that Shape Your Worlds: Global, National, and Local
Millennium Project. http://www.millennium-project.org. The section titled "15 Global Challenges"

Chapter 7 Events that Will Change Your Business
Schwartz, Peter. *The Art of the Long View.* New York: Currency Doubleday, 1991.

Chapter 8 The Two-Axis Matrix
Jaquith, Andrew, *Security Metrics: Replacing Fear, Uncertainty, and Doubt.* Boston: Addison-Wesley Professional, 2007.
Van der Heijden, Kees, *Scenarios* (p. 247 "The matrix approach"). John Wiley & Sons Chichester, 2006.

Chapter 9 Your Business: Strengths, Weaknesses, Opportunities, and Threats
Glenn, Jerome C. and Gordon, Theodore J. eds. *Futures Research Methodology,* Washington: American Council for the United Nations University, 2009.

Chapter 10 Scenarios: How futurists Explore Alternate Futures
Bezold, Clem. "Aspirational Futures." Journal of Futures Studies, vol. 13, no. 4 (2009) 81-90.
Gordon, Adam. *Future Savvy.* New York: AMACOM, 2009.
Inayatullah, Sohail. "Six Pillars: futures thinking for transforming." Foresight, vol. 10, no. 1 (2008) 4-21.
Kaivo-oja, Jari. "Scenario Learning and Potential Sustainable Development Processes in Spatial Contexts: Towards Risk Society or Ecological Modernization Scenarios." Futures Research Quarterly, vol. 17, no. 2, (2001) 33-55.
Lao Tzu   www.brainyquote.com/quotes/lao_tzu_130286
Link, Ed. "Link Trainer"
https://en.wikipedia.org/wiki/Link_Trainer
Sunstein, Cass R. *Worst Case Scenarios.* Cambridge: Harvard University Press

Van der Heijden, Kees. *Scenarios*. West Sussex: John Wiley & Sons, Ltd., 2006.

Chapter 11 Building Your Basic Scenario

Chermack, Thomas J., Lynham, Susan A. and Ruona, Wendy E. "A Review of Scenario Planning Literature". Futures Research Quarterly, vol. 17, no. 2, (2001) 7-31.
Lindberg, Charles. "Charles Lindberg". Wikipedia https://en.wikipedia.org/wiki/Charles_Lindbergh. **Accessed 2019.**

Chapter 12 Driving Forces Will Change the Direction of Your Scenarios

Taleb, Nassim Nicholas. *The Black Swan*. New York: Random House, 2007.

Chapter 13 Telling Stories about the Future of Your Business

Cascio, Jamais. "Futures Thinking: Writing Scenarios". Fast Company. http://www.fastcompany.com/1560416/futures-thinking-writing-scenarios. (03/15/10).
Shell. "Scenarios". https://www.shell.com/energy-and-innovation/the-energy-future/scenarios/what-are-scenarios.html.
Shell. "Older scenarios". https://www.shell.com/energy-and-innovation/the-energy-future/scenarios/new-lenses-on-the-future/earlier-scenarios.html..

Chapter 14 Strategic Planning for Small Business

Mintzberg, Henry, Ahlstrand, Bruce and Lampel, Joseph. *Strategy Safari*. New York: The Free Press, 1998.
.

Chapter 15 A Vision of the Future of Your Small Business
Senge, Peter and others. The Fifth Discipline: The Art and
Practice of the Learning Organization. New York: Doubleday,
1990.

Chapter 16 Strategies to Achieve your Vision
De Geus, Arie. P. "Planning as Learning." Harvard Business
Review, no. March-April (1988): 70-74.
Goodstein, L. D., Nolan, T. M. and Pfeiffer, J. W. *Applied Strategic
Planning.* San Francisco: Pfeiffer & Company, 1992.
Mintzberg, Henry. *The Rise and Fall of Strategic Planning.* New York:
Free Press, 1994.
Dixit, Anash K. and Nalekuff, Barry J. *Thinking Strategically.* New
York: W.W. Norton, 1991.

Chapter 17 Creating an Action Plan
Hines, Andy and Bishop, Peter, ed. *Thinking About the Future.*
Washington, DC: Social Technologies, 2006.
Pofeldt, Elaine. The Million-Dollar One-Person Business. New
York:
Lorena Jones Books, 2018

Chapter 18 Analyzing Your Plan
Hines, Andy and Bishop, Peter, ed. *Thinking About the Future.*
Washington, DC: Social Technologies, 2006

Chapter 19 Wild Cards and Contingency Plans
Barber, Marcus. "Wildcards—Signals from a Future Near You".
Journal of Futures Studies, vol. 11, no. 1, (2006), 75-94.
Peterson, John L. *Out of the Blue.* Arlington: Arlington Institute,
1997.
Taleb, Nassim Nicholas. *The Black Swan.* New York: Random
House, 2007.

Chapter 20 Living With Your Plan

Wheelwright, Verne. *Small Business Foresight Workbook*. Harlingen: Personal Futures Network, www.personalfutures.net. 2006.

Chapter 21 The Long Term Perspective

Kouzes, James M. and Posner, Barry Z. *The Leadership Challenge*, San Francisco: Jossey Bass/Pfeiffer, 2002.

Meadows, D. H. *Thinking in Systems*. White River Junction VT.: Chelsea Green, 2008.

Index

The Author

 Verne Wheelwright has worked in small business for most of his life. He went back to school and earned a Master's degree in Studies of the Future at the University of Houston (Clear Lake) then, convinced that there was a need, began research in personal futures for his Ph.D. dissertation. This book, *Small Business Foresight,* along with his book, *It's YOUR Future... Make it a Good One!* and their companion workbooks are results of that research.

Wheelwright was convinced that the foresight methods that have been so successful for businesses and governments worldwide should work for individuals and small businesses as well. His broad background in small business and international business combined with his travels to much of the world have provided him with a strong foundation for his futures research, and added an understanding of cultural and economic differences that affect people's lives and businesses.

Wheelwright has tested his work in presentations and workshops with business people of different ages and varied cultural backgrounds, with gratifying results. He continues to receive expressions of gratitude from people who have read his books or articles or visited his web site at www.smallbusinessforesight.com. Wheelwright plans to continue his research, speaking and writing about personal and small business futures.

Verne is a Charter member of the Association of Professional Futurists, and a Fellow in the World Futures Studies Federation.

CPSIA information can be obtained
at www.ICGtesting.com
Printed in the USA
BVHW040749031019
560088BV00003B/10/P

9 780989 263573